TOTALLY DRIVEN
My Incurable Journey

Totally Driven
My Incurable Journey

SUSIE CORNELL MBE,
DEPUTY LIEUTENANT OF ESSEX,

*INTERNATIONAL NATURAL HEALTH,
BIORESONANCE CONSULTANT*

Text Carole Richardson, on behalf of Story Terrace

Design Grade Design and Adeline Media, London

Copyright © Susie Cornell: 2019

ISBN 9781916307100 (ebook)

ISBN 9781916307117 (paperback)

Publisher: The Cornell Centre Publication

www.susiecornell.com

Story Terrace

www.StoryTerrace.com

CONTENTS

PREFACE

While visiting a garden centre, I found myself drawn to a plant with white leaves that I'd never seen before. After learning that it was called 'Angel Wings', I took it home with me. That evening, my beloved mum died. And I knew then that it was time for me to write my story...

Me and my mum

1

LIFE IN THE FAST LANE

Wearing a big smile and a skimpy bikini, I suddenly find myself strutting along a golden beach in glorious sunshine. The year is 1972, and I am a world away from Kitts Green in the Majorcan resort of Palma Nova. Nobody I know back home has even been to Majorca before, let alone worked here!

My job is that of a beach party seller for the Barbarella Discotheque Night Boat Party, which means that the warm, soft sands and the turquoise Mediterranean Sea are my workplace. My office, if you like, furnished with cypress and olive trees, sunbeds, parasols and pedalos.

Not a bad life at all, I'm thinking when my attention is suddenly drawn to a group of girls clustered around one sunbed. Talk about bees round a honeypot! On closer inspection I see that the object of their fascination is a boy from our apartment block, one Mr George Best. He spots me, and instantly flashes that famous smile and waves, so I wave back, acknowledging the handsome young talented

George Best on the beach of Palma Nova

footballer from Belfast. Celebrities are everywhere you look.

In Birmingham, it would probably be damp, despite being early summer, and I'd be catching the number 14 bus into the city, desperately seeking out a bit of glamour amongst the sooty, industrial surroundings. In sparkling Majorca, it was all on my doorstep. And what a doorstep! I could wake up in the apartment I shared with Sue and Sonia, who'd travelled out with me, and take a short stroll to the beach to 'work' whilst looking across a horizon littered with powerboats and yachts. One of those yachts moored there belonged to the entrepreneur Freddie Laker, I'd heard, not realising that I'd be attending parties aboard it soon enough. For the first time in my life, I was free to be me; to do what I pleased.

But I was in Birmingham, it was 1971 and I was sashaying down the garden path in my canary yellow hot pants suit and white knee high boots, I am met by a crowd of neighbours gathered on the kerb.

Agog, a dozen pairs of eyes flit from me to the flashy yellow Lotus Europa parked on the street. It might as well have been a spaceship that's landed; it's so out of place there.

I like this, I smile to myself, lapping up all the celebrity worthy attention I'm getting as I sink into the leather passenger seat. *I could get used to it.*

It was the early seventies and I was 19 or 20, still living in the family home on a Birmingham council estate and working as a newspaper secretary and fashion model.

My date for the evening was James whose father was the owner of an upmarket garage hence the expensive sport car that perfectly, though quite coincidentally, matched the colour of my outfit.

If he was surprised to see the modest background that I came from, James didn't show it. Our family car was a Morris Minor and we didn't even have a telephone in our house. So when he'd asked for my phone number, I'd had to give him one for Mrs Webb, a neighbour of ours who lived across the road. When the call came, one of her five children ran over to get me. It was a community service she carried out for all the neighbours as hers was the only phone on the street.

"You must live in a very big house; it took you so long to get to the phone," James said when, breathless and still wearing my slippers, I finally reached the receiver.

I hadn't corrected him and he was too much of a gentleman to bring it up when he pulled up outside our red brick semi to sweep me off to a more affluent area of the city than Kitts Green Road. Our paths had only crossed in the first place because I'd been doing some promotion work for his father's garage, draping my petite frame across sports car bonnets to imitate - albeit more modestly the famous Pirelli calendar.

Tonight wasn't about work though, this was pleasure of an alien nature to me, whizzing along the city's roads in the kind of car that didn't belong to my district. I'd never experienced anything like it before. It was exciting!

I like this moments; they're nice, I told myself.

Stourbridge was the sort of place where Lotus sports cars belonged, and I'm pretty sure that's where he took me. Probably back to the pub where a crowd of people like him used to meet up. Some of them became my friends too, like James' best friend Peter Powell, who'd just become a DJ for Radio Luxembourg and who'd later move on to Radio One and marry the TV presenter Anthea Turner. I'm still in touch with Peter today and his cousin, Puddy, who he introduced me to, became a very close friend, as did Anthea.

Although I was never ashamed of my roots and never made any attempt to hide where I came from, there was no denying that I was being introduced to a new and entirely different lifestyle to my own. And, proud as I was of my loving family and where I lived, I was instantly seduced by it. James couldn't have realised it any more than I did at the time, but when he opened the door of that showstopping car for me, he was giving me access to another, far more glamorous existence than the working class one that I knew. Life in the fast lane. And I would soon love every minute of it. There was no going back.

2

HUMBLE BEGINNINGS

As fast as my little seven-year-old legs can carry me, I'm running out of the school gate, desperate to share my exciting news with my waiting mum.

"Mummy, Mummy, you need to make me a crown of flowers!" I instruct her.

"What are you talking about?" she wants to know, slightly puzzled by my request.

"They want me to be the May Queen!" I manage to blurt out before the emotion of it all take over and I promptly burst into floods of tears. The year is 1958 and this is one of my earliest memories, indicating just how excited I felt at such a young age to be picked out of the crowd and thrust into the spotlight.

Even though our school – Lea Village Primary – had never had a May Queen before and never has since, May Day celebrations were a huge event in working class communities in the midlands and the north. It was probably more than just coincidence that my own mum was a florist when the teachers chose me, but nevertheless nothing was going to spoil my moment of glory – not even the jealousy of all the other mothers, who felt the honour should have gone to their daughters! And when the Big Day came, I couldn't have been happier as I sat, resplendent in my white dress and floral crown, head and shoulders above my classmates, feted by the crowd. Sitting right behind me was my proud mum with my nan and sister Yvonne.

'Queen of the May' picture

Looking back, you could argue that it was my first taste of a more glamorous life than the very ordinary one I was born into when I entered the world on April 23rd, 1951. And it instantly fascinated me. The eldest daughter of Albert and Olive (known fondly as Topsy, my father's pet name for her) Mills, our first family home was a terraced house on King Edward Road. Yvonne followed me four years later and then along came Kim and Tracey when I was 12. Four girls! As the eldest, I was my mother's special helper, feeding, changing nappies and looking after the babies. Those domestic duties were my way of life and I loved it.

Our family lived on the main road in Kitts Green, a road often called the 'Horse Road'; it was on the main bus route, a 20-minute bus ride into the city centre. Just a few minutes' walk from our house there was a parade of shops and my school. Dad was a long-distance lorry driver for Chad Valley Toys, which might explain why, when I was 18 months old, I got my special teddy Growler, who was bigger than me. Mum, who was more creative and artistic, worked from home doing flowers for weddings and funerals. Life there was happy, if not affluent. I was loved and adored by both my parents, and one of the few times I can remember being told off was for eating the cement between the house bricks, believe it or not! I've no idea why I did it, but I loved it so much that I even got a stool to get to the higher bricks. When I'd eaten all the cement I could reach, I went to our next door neighbour's house with the stool and started doing the same. Realising it

Me, John and my sister Kim at our house in Kitts Green

wasn't my own home, I gave up. Even though they were built together, it must have tasted different!

My mum and my dad meant the whole world to me, as did my wonderful nan (my dad's mum). Not uncommonly for the working classes in that era, she lived with us and I shared a double bed with her. Often, in the middle of the night, I'd wake up with pains in my legs that my mum had said were growing pains. My nan would tenderly massage my legs, but it never seemed to help. I can't help but wonder, today, whether it was an early sign of the medical problem that was to later emerge and change the entire course of my life. Who can say…

In an attempt to address the problem, my mum sent me off to dancing classes for tap and ballet and it was a win-win. I loved dancing, even gaining a silver medal and taking the leading role in a showcase performance at Birmingham Hippodrome – and it seemed to cure my leg pains.

Me, Yvonne and Mum at the seaside

Off stage, my ordinary life continued, and during the school holidays when I was eight, Dad woke me very early in the morning so as not to disturb the others in the house. He'd ask me to get dressed, and after breakfast he'd help me into the high cab of his huge lorry, already loaded up. I felt like Santa's special helper, delivering all those toys. We'd spend the driving time playing I Spy and singing lots of songs, many verses of 'One Man Went to Mow' and enthusiastic renditions of 'She'll Be Coming Round the Mountain When She Comes'. The lorry was basic, there was no radio for entertainment or communication, but the fact that my dad had chosen me to go on these trips made me feel extra special.

I had a good relationship with my father. Sometimes he'd take me with him up the road and ask me to wait outside a green shop with the sign 'Turf Accountant' over the door while he went inside. He seemed to be in there ages, and much to the confusion of my young mind, we never got any new grass for the garden. On other occasions, he'd give me some money wrapped up in white paper and send me up the road to see a 'man about a dog'. I had to do this every Sunday morning, but a new dog never appeared. Years later it dawned on me why Dad was so brilliant at maths, readily doing any calculations in his head. Working out all those betting odds must have been good practice!

Many more happy hours were spent pressing wildflowers with my nan between the pages of the family Bible, and another book she loved, John Bunyan's *Pilgrim's Progress*.

Sadly, those books were all I was given to remind me of my nan after she died, and only then because nobody else wanted them. Having worked in the jewellery quarter in Birmingham throughout her life, she'd collected some beautiful jewellery, including lots of earrings. When she asked me to put them into her pierced ears, I couldn't do it because I thought I would hurt her! She also had so many necklaces with diamonds and rubies that I was sure she'd been a gypsy in her early life. (Recently I had a hereditary DNA scan and I am 0.8 per cent Egyptian, so there may be a connection somewhere!) I never received any of it as my aunties took the jewellery away and divided it up. I avoided them after that episode.

My growing taste for the finer things in life was only honed with visits to my father's older sister, Jess, who was a huge influence on my life. She and my uncle Baxter owned a hotel called the Corner House in Scotland, an old and impressive building that dated back to 1760, placed on the wide high street of the seaside town of Montrose, on the east coast. I'd go up and spend the long summer holidays with them between the ages of nine to 11. My aunt and uncle had no children of their own, so they treated me like a daughter, indulging me with horse riding lessons and introducing me to influential guests and locals. My sister Yvonne was invited too but she didn't want to go because it meant leaving our mum. Much as I too loved my mum, I also loved this other lifestyle.

The height of the hotel day was afternoon high tea, and I had never experienced anything like it. I was mesmerised by the waitresses humming around the dining room in their black dresses and little white aprons and hats. Auntie Jess taught me a lot about etiquette, including how to lay the table and how to sit properly, but the best part of the day was being able to slide down the banister and to sit in the cocktail bar when everyone had gone home. She encouraged me to work in the kitchen alongside the staff, who taught me how to make butter balls and lay out the trays for room service. I was learning so much about the hotel industry and seeing another side of life and I loved every minute of it. Auntie Jess let me dine with the adults and made me walk up and down the beautiful spiral staircase with a pile of books balanced on the top of my head.

The Corner House Hotel

"It's good for your deportment," she would say, as if I were at a unique finishing school. "It will help you later in life." Years later, she was to be proved right when modelling called for good posture.

As I approached my 11th birthday, she asked my mother if I could go and live at the Corner House. Mum said no, that she and Dad needed me home because my little sister Yvonne was missing me so much. I'm sure she would also rather have had me at home than living so far away in Scotland. Her refusal ended my holidays to Montrose. Our only contact after this was by telephone. When I visited the town recently, the hotel was derelict and in need of complete refurbishment. It was an emotional moment, seeing somewhere that held a special place in my childhood so neglected.

Ever the sensitive soul (I used to cry my eyes out when I watched *Lassie* and *Fury the Wonder Horse* on TV), I couldn't bear to see any animal hurt. I still can't. Our home was full of pets – cats, dogs, rabbits, hamsters, gerbils and budgies. When any passed away I performed their funerals. I'd invite the children down the road to be pall bearers, carrying the dead pets with pomp and ceremony to be buried, making an occasion of the event. I loved animals so much. When given an autograph book for one birthday and not then knowing any famous people who could sign it, I used to dip the paw of my newborn kittens in a special mud mixture and imprint them on the pages along with their names. To me they were important enough to be famous!

My cat was always having kittens and I would have to find homes for them – though not for one grey haired beauty. Silver was special. And when she was six weeks old, in my desperation to show her off I took her to visit a neighbour's house. As I played on the hearth rug with her, my neighbour's daughter was doing her hair in front of the mirror above the fireplace. All of a sudden, she stepped back and her stiletto heel when straight through Silver's neck. Amidst screams and shouts, I went into total shock. At some point a man arrived with a big bucket of water and it was the last I saw of poor Silver.

My mum used to worry about me being so sensitive. She didn't think that I had enough confidence, and to address that the answer lay in drama classes at the secondary school that was not of my choosing. Or my mother's.

Like so many others, I didn't pass the 11 plus exam for the local grammar school. It's no surprise really. *Pilgrim's Progress* and the Bible made up two of the only three books we had in our house. The other was the doctor's encyclopaedia. Dad would buy me *The Dandy, Beano* and *Bunty* comics though, so we had some variation in our reading material! There were no local libraries for borrowing books.

Nevertheless, my mother was horrified: she didn't want me going to the local secondary modern as she thought it would limit my opportunities.

"You're not going to the sec modern. You're better than that," she'd insist as I cried myself to sleep every night, feeling like my whole world had come to an end.

So she fought tooth and nail to get me into Sir Wilfrid's Martineau Bilateral school in Tile Cross, Birmingham. It was neither a grammar nor a secondary modern and competed with its neighbours on its own terms.

When I started at Sir Wilfrid's I was immediately put in the C stream because I hadn't passed the 11 plus, but by the end of the term I'd been promoted to the A stream, where I was allowed to study algebra and Chaucer. It was a shock to encounter a new mathematical language, something I'd never been exposed to previously, but I got on with it as best I could.

Despite a wobbly start, when the first book I was told to read there was *The Lost World* by Sir Arthur Conan Doyle and I cried every night because I found it so difficult, I discovered that my heart really lay with English and drama lessons. I could often be found in the drama class or volunteering to read the prayers in assembly. I was really beginning to enjoy an audience by this stage, and my mum was right when she said it would do my confidence the world of good. It did. I loved art, chemistry and biology too, but developed a hatred of maths. It was soon clear that I hadn't inherited my father's talent for numbers. An added bonus was a school trip to Italy – my first taste of life abroad – at the age of 14. Flying back then was rare and hugely expensive, so we travelled all the way by coach.

Back home, life continued in the same way for the first two or three years of my secondary education. Animals

Sixth Form day out in London

were still everywhere, including a new and unusual one: a monkey with no tail! One night, my dad just walked through the door with Patsy sitting on his shoulder. She was roughly the size of the monkeys that could be found sitting on top of barrel organs during variety acts, and I was fascinated by her. I could sit and study her tiny hands for hours, amazed by how similar they were to my own human hands. Most of the time Patsy stuck to my dad, but we made a home for her under the sink unit and she took to sleeping there. During the day she was allowed outside on a long lead and ran along the clothesline in the garden or climbed around the house. Eventually, she learned how to get onto the chimney of our neighbour's house; she only came down when my dad got home from work. On another occasion, my friend came to visit and put her engagement ring on top of the sink while she washed her hands. Patsy stole the ring and put it in her mouth. She kept teasing us, showing us the ring, but wouldn't give it back. My poor friend was in in tears all day, until my dad came home and Patsy handed the ring over to him no problem. She was especially close to my dad and would sit and preen him as soon as he got in from work. Mum dressed Patsy in frilly dresses and nappies. It was the time when chimps were advertising Typhoo tea on TV; my aunt was a 'tea taster's assistant' there, so perhaps that's where we got the idea from. Nearby Drayton Manor had chimps' tea parties too, so to us it seemed perfectly normal to dress Patsy up and treat her as one of the family.

She lived with us until she died of pneumonia after I'd fled the nest.

Saturday nights out were spent sitting in my dad's brother's charabanc coach, sliding around on the bench seats with no seat belts to secure us. My uncle had seven children and we'd share our crisps and pork scratchings with them, drinking glass bottles of orange fizzy Tizer and having a great time on days out to Drayton Manor. By the time I was 14, I had taken to wearing false eyelashes, which I would curl carefully on the sofa as I applied them. My sisters rushed back and forth getting ready for bed in their bri-nylon nighties, generating so much static that it acted as a magnet to my nylon eyelashes, which attached to their nighties. I had to chase them around the house, shouting, "Come here and give me my eyelashes back! They're stuck on your nighties again!"

Music was, and still is, a huge part of my life (and career for a time). I loved Motown and the Beatles and grew up with their songs throughout my adolescent years. When they were due to appear in Birmingham, I begged and pleaded my parents to get a ticket. Dad dropped my friends and me off outside the Odeon on New Street at five in the morning so that we could join the queue and get our tickets. When I went to the show I could neither hear nor see the Beatles because of the screaming audience – I was screaming along too, through my tears. I cried all the way there and back. My mother was so upset that I was in such a state but they were tears of happiness: I was so happy to have seen the Beatles live. Little did I ever think that years later I'd meet the closest thing to Paul McCartney – his dad!

Life wasn't all hunky dory in my teens, though – as it tends not to be – and soon my mum and dad seemed to be rowing. A lot. My baby sisters, Kim and Tracey, were only two and three at the time, and I can remember sitting at the top of the stairs with my older sister Yvonne, holding her tightly while trying to reassure her that everything would be OK. I blamed myself and thought they were rowing over me, without knowing why. It felt as if everything was my fault. Maybe I'd done something wrong? Maybe I was adopted? I even searched the house for paperwork that might back that theory up but, of course, found nothing.

Eventually my mum told us that we were going to live with my nan. I was 14 at the time and both Yvonne and I were told we'd have to miss school for the moment. The thought of missing my friends made me sad.

Out of the blue, Dad turned up to take Yvonne and Kim with him. Mum, who was holding Tracey in her arms, was screaming. I was screaming. But to no avail. Bundling them into his lorry, he drove off and there was nothing we could do about it. Missing my sisters became a real trauma.

My nan had only one room for us to share. My granddad lived a couple of doors away but I never knew why. Opposite was a builder's yard where a boy I got to know called Geoffrey worked. As a Mod, he drove a scooter with lots of mirrors and lights. Needless to say I was infatuated. He used to play the Beach Boys hit 'God Only Knows' for me and I still think of him to this day when I hear that song.

Inside the house, life was less glamorous. My auntie Janet lived with us and we only had a tin bath between us all. The outside toilet down the alley was accessible only by torch and the loo roll was old newspaper!

Mum, finding it difficult to live like this, took us back home to Dad and my other two sisters. It's a vivid memory as the television screen was dominated by news coverage of the terrible Aberfan disaster in 1966. I was utterly heartbroken. Falling back into routine, I would kiss both my mum and dad goodnight in an attempt to return to normality. But it was never the same. Little familiar things that had created the love and security I'd previously felt were lost. Like my mum's name. Dad no longer called her by his term of endearment, Topsy. She was now firmly Olive. And, never for a minute imagining the romantic heartbreak that I would myself go on to cause, that really hurt me.

3

FIRST LOVE, FIRST HEARTBREAK

The atmosphere is buzzing in The Locarno Ballroom on Hurst Street, Birmingham and, aged sweet 16, I am lapping it up. Underneath the huge, sparkly glitter ball, I am twisting the night away to the sounds of the Beatles, the Beach Boys and the Monkees with the happy crowds.

It is the late '60s and life's good! England is still on a high after winning the world cup in 1966, beating West Germany with that famous last-minute goal from Geoff Hurst. Even with no interest in football, I'd been as excited as everyone else as I watched that legendary cup final at the hair salon where I worked on Saturdays, sweeping up and learning how to set, perm and tint. I knew hairdressing wasn't the career for me though.

What I didn't know then was that among the crowds on the ballroom's sprung, polished dance floor, I was about to find and fall for my very own professional footballer. His name was John and he was apprenticed to West Bromwich Albion. Oh the glamour!

I was still at school at the time, where I stayed on into the sixth form, learning shorthand and typing to equip myself for secretarial work. My aunt was a tea taster's assistant at Typhoo tea in Birmingham, and in my school holidays I worked in that factory environment, a responsible role where I had to clock in every morning. It was my first taste of working life, the first time I had mixed with older women, and I certainly started to learn the facts of life from them. So after gaining my secretarial qualifications, I left school at 18. It was an emotional moment as I'd loved my time there. Perhaps sensing my ambitions, the headmaster bought me a rosebush called 'Superstar' which was planted in the front garden at home. (Believe it or not, it is still blooming there after all these years.)

Armed with a fresh bunch of certificates, I started work for the managing director of Herbert Controls and Instruments, a member of BSA group, which was a big manufacturing company in Birmingham. I didn't stay in the job long – I was looking for a more glamorous career.

For a while I worked in the middle of the city in the management office of the newly opened Bullring Shopping Centre. Whilst working there, I was presented to Princess Anne on her official visit to Birmingham to open a bridge, a new link between the Bullring and New Street Station. It was quite an event and my first, but not last, contact with royalty.

Then I got a job that changed the direction of my life. I worked as secretary for the women's fashion editor of the

Modeling for the Birmingham Post *newspaper, aged 20, 1971*

SUE MILLS

Height 5'5
Bust 34 Waist 24 Hips 36
Shoes 5 Gloves 7
Hair : dark brown
Eyes : grey/green

TELECAST STUDIOS
14 Navigation St.
Birmingham 2.
021.643.8528

Birmingham Post and *Mail*, Barbara Crossette. She was an American writer who went on to write for the USA papers and became a United Nations correspondent and a freelance writer on foreign policy. A formidable journalist who I respected and enjoyed working with. I found the world of fashion fascinating, so when the paper encouraged me do a modelling course with Telecast on Navigation Street, I was keen to take it up. I became the in-house photographic model at the *Birmingham Post*, modelling many of the clothes for their feature articles, including one for a 'dashing full-sleeved blouse in washable white crepe at £8.' It was 1971. I changed my look in order to be different, wore miniskirts and another item of clothing that was all the rage in the early '70's: hot pants. I was so comfortable in those extra-short shorts that I entered the Miss Barbarella Hot Pants Competition, judged by the star comedian Jimmy Tarbuck. I came second.

Modelling gave me the taste of glamour I craved, and the experience of a different way of life that led me into these new social circles. It was John who encouraged me to enter the Miss Birmingham City beauty contest, which I won. This automatically entered me into the Miss Jersey Holiday Queen contest. I had to tell my mum and dad about my competition win and my trip to Jersey. I'd never been on a plane before. John came with me and stayed nearby as all the girls were put together in the four-star luxury Hotel De France in St Helier. I shared a room with Lee Hamilton,

Entering the Jersey Holiday Queen contest as Miss Birmingham

who won the competition and became Miss Scotland and was automatically entered into Miss England. The beauty competitions made a big impression on me; they had catapulted me into a different world, with different people. It was a world I had never experienced before, but I liked it and I wanted more. I was still unsure of what I wanted to do with my life though, or which career path to follow. I was just happy living in the moment I was in. We lived near Birmingham Airport and I'd always been fascinated by it. At night, I was mesmerised by the bright lights on the runway and always wondered where they might take me. Something was telling me I had to get on a plane and go somewhere. Follow the lights.

I got my chance on a night out with friends at the Opposite Lock nightclub in Birmingham in 1971, when we were approached by one of the guys who worked there,

"Hi girls, do you fancy a job selling beach party tickets in Majorca?" he asked. Leave grey and industrial Birmingham for the beach glamour and sun? I didn't have to think about it for too long. Not wanting to worry my parents, I told them that I was going on holiday and when I got to Majorca, I wrote and said I was staying for a while longer. Any upset they might have felt was much less than the pain I caused John though. He had asked me to marry him and I'd broken his heart when I'd said I wanted to move on without him. In a way it would have been easier to get married than to let him down and hurt him so badly. It taught me a lot: never fall in love until the right time and with the right person. It was so painful to break up with him and it destroyed John, who later followed me to Majorca, bringing a girl who looked just like me. By then I was certain I had made the right decision to move to another life, leaving behind the trauma that our relationship had already caused me...

At 17, I'd been menstruating regularly for about four years and I'd been able to set the clock by my periods from the word go. They came every 28 days, often on the hour. So when one month nothing happened, I was confused. I waited another week but still nothing. A friend handed me three pills with the promise they would start my period. I took them, but still nothing happened.

Could I be pregnant? I wondered. Naively, I didn't think this could be possible as nothing much had really happened between us sexually, had it? Or maybe it had? I was confused, frightened and thoroughly ashamed. These were very different days that we were living in, and getting pregnant out of wedlock was viewed as shameful. I knew it would destroy my mum and dad, who still had two young daughters to bring up. And I also had another fear, that I would be sent away and never see them again. It wasn't a fear based on wild imaginings: my friend Pamela had been a victim of the times. I used to visit her often, but one day I went round to see her and her older sister answered the door to tell me that Pamela had gone to stay in Wales with family to have a baby.

"She probably won't come back here," she added.

To me, it was a huge shock hearing that I'd never see my friend again. And now, I felt sure that I would face the same fate if my pregnancy continued. I couldn't speak about it to anyone, not even John. It was my body and my problem. It was up to me to deal with it. There was no way I could even visit our family doctor. I had nowhere to turn.

Then one day, I was flicking through *Cosmopolitan* magazine and saw an advertisement for the Brook Street Advisory Centre. One had just opened in Birmingham, so I booked an appointment and went along. Not knowing what they were going ask or what they could do, I discovered that they could make me an appointment for an abortion in London the following week. It would cost £100 – an absolute fortune in those days. And although I didn't see how I had any choice, I didn't have any money. And neither did John. After John's apprenticeship finished at West Brom, he'd failed to win a place in the team. And in those days, that meant there was little future. He was now 18 and had put his all into that football apprenticeship, even leaving school early, and with no other training behind him, he wasn't equipped for any other career. As a result of this, he'd turned to petty theft, getting himself caught and sent away to a detention centre for three months early on in our relationship. Distraught, I'd cried myself to sleep every night that he was away.

Somehow, though, we managed to scrape together the necessary £100 and headed for St John's Wood in London, where the clinic was. John came with me and so did two of my friends. While they waited outside, I was led, terrified, into a private room. I had absolutely no idea what to expect and when asked if I wanted an explanation of what would happen, I answered, "No."

The next thing I remember is waking up afterwards and being told that I could go home to Birmingham. Still we didn't talk about it. But a month after the operation, John and I were getting off the bus at the top of our road when I started bleeding profusely. It was so bad I couldn't move, and John had to run and get my dad. Arriving with his arms full of blankets, he wrapped me up in them and took me home. No questions were asked.

Years on, I do still feel for young women like myself who had to go through with abortions. In the circumstances at that time, I had no choice, like so many others. I would have destroyed my loving family and I couldn't do that. I doubt people today would understand just how strong the restraints of that time were. Given what nature had in store for me where babies were concerned, though, I do often think, *Is God paying me back for what I did? Is it payback?*

But I can't allow myself to think like that. I've had to let go of it. I cannot go down that road.

4

BIRMINGHAM SUE IS BORN

was young and flying high. I'd recently celebrated my
21st birthday in my apartment, where only the huge
bunch of red roses sent over from 'a mystery admirer' in
England had made me think fleetingly of home and what I
was 'missing'.

Outside the bright, exotic bubble I was now living in,
the world was a very serious place: the Vietnam War was
still going on; Watergate had happened and the Troubles
were brewing in Northern Ireland. Lord knows, we needed
the newly launched first BBC 'pop' station, Radio One, to
lighten the load. As much as Birmingham needed the final
stretch of the M6 that had just opened north of Spaghetti
Junction.

My 21st birthday at my apartment in Majorca with fellow beach party ticket sellers

After the Beatles had parted company, I'd switched some of my musical allegiance to Carly Simon. And her song 'You're so vain' was a fitting backdrop to my life on that magical island. Working hard and playing hard, I was surrounded by interesting and vibrant people everywhere, many of whom were celebrities. Although high-rise hotels were sprouting along the south coast of the island, near Magaluf, Palma Nova remained relatively unspoilt and elite back then. It was a place to see and be seen. Cheap package holidays didn't take off until later in the '70s, and a holiday abroad was regarded as an exotic treat out of reach for my very ordinary family. Working abroad was unheard of. It made me different. Unique, exciting! Boarding that plane at Birmingham Airport had changed my life beyond recognition. And it was about to change again...

Despite the glamorous surroundings, we were living hand-to-mouth and earning very little. As official sellers, our job was to parade the beach touting our tickets in our bikini 'uniforms' with Barbarella Boat Party badges proudly pinned to them. Nice work but low pay: we relied on commission from our sales to eat. And unfortunately, tragedy existed even in paradise, as we discovered to our poor friends' cost.

We'd befriended the Glaswegian couple in the flat next door, Ian and Evelyn, who were engaged and selling boat party tickets like us. Although Ian came from a wealthy family with a bakery business in Glasgow, he wanted to make his own way in life and worked 24-7 selling his tickets, taking every opportunity he could. Occasionally boat party trips went to hidden caves, only accessible by water. We didn't go on them as we thought they would be too dangerous, but Ian did. The boat party music was so loud it dislodged one of the rocks in the ceiling of the cave. As it fell, it hit poor Ian, killing him instantly. The caves were closed and Evelyn returned to Glasgow after that. Shocked, we mourned the death of our friend, but had no choice but to continue in our jobs in order to survive.

Although Ian wasn't forgotten, life carried on for us and we still managed to enjoy some of the island's nightlife, attending a handful of special places alongside worldwide celebrities. There was Tito's, a refined cabaret club where Frank Sinatra and Frankie Vaughan frequently performed, and we often went on the boat party rides to the Barbarella nightclub.

Amongst the places to be seen on Majorca, Ricki's Bar was where you went to have a drink, to be noticed, to shine bright among the 'in crowd.' A guy I knew in Palma Nova worked for a travel company and invited me for drinks there one evening; I was more than happy to go. Ricki's was a bar called 'My Own Place' – 'MOP', a glamorous, luxury cocktail lounge, the Studio 54 of the island, perched on a clifftop overlooking the bay.

Inside it was nothing short of opulent. Furnished with mirrored tables, studded leather columns and velvet sofas, the low, white building had huge windows and a glass bar up on the roof. I took a seat with my drink and stared all around me. The night-time view over the bay below was nothing short of spectacular. All twinkling lights, fancy hotels and boats. So that was why everyone flocked to Ricki's!

As soon as we arrived, Ricki rushed over and introduced himself. Ricki 'Lash' Lazzar was the American owner; his radio station, Radio Majorca, broadcast from the bar every night. It was the only English-speaking radio station in the whole of Spain. Ricki also wrote a daily column for the *Majorca Bulletin*, something he would do for 45 years. He looked like a '70s version of Puck from *A Midsummer Night's Dream*, with his goatee beard and twinkling smile. A socialiser and promotor, he was often to be found with a cigar and trademark sunglasses. Less than an hour later, he came back to speak to me.

"Sue, do you fancy coming to work for me? You could be a DJ, playing music and doing the adverts for the live radio station we have here, Radio Majorca."

"But I've never worked on the radio!" I replied, stunned. This information didn't seem to faze Ricki, "I'll teach you! I'll teach you everything you need to know," he promised. And he did. Soon I was the first female DJ they had ever had. In the right place at the right time. As soon as Ricki discovered I was from Birmingham, he nicknamed me 'Birmingham Sue'. He would tease me on the radio that he had picked me up from a coal mine in Birmingham and sent me to elocution lessons, which always made me laugh.

Ricki's was the place to be on the island. Everybody who was anybody would drink there – pop stars, singers like Frankie Vaughan, entrepreneurs including Freddie Laker (who took us night fishing in the Bay of Palma, where the crew cooked us breakfast and Freddie taught me how to water ski – I couldn't swim, so unsurprisingly I didn't pursue that sport. There were many parties on his yacht and he became a good friend). George Best was also a regular at Ricki's, and he was always surrounded by a bevy of besotted women. In light of my taxi experience, perhaps they were paying his way…

Birmingham Sue live on Radio Majorca with Ricki Lash

THE 'RIKI LASH' LAZAAR SHOW

HOWDY AMIGOS.
Let's get on that diet! On second thoughts, forget it, New Year's Eve is on its way.

THE ACHIEVER!

TROOPS,
The Lash on many occasions refers to a former disc jockey on one of the original Radio Mallorca programmes when she broadcast from the MOP (My Own Place) those many years ago.

Sue was a vivacious lady with film star looks, who gained immediate popularity as she should have done, being the first lady in all of Spain, broadcasting nightly from a celeb bar five hours a night from 7 till midnight in English. Oh yes, she was the belle of the ball, so to speak, and many a fella had a crush on Birmingham Sue.

So after a few seasons, Sue, a successful model in Great Britain before she decided to have an adventure in Majorca to get away form all that, decided to the sadness of her fans to return home.

Sue, with her looks, was right smack back into the modelling scene, but then tragedy struck as she became afflicted with Multiple Sclerosis.

Those of us who know people afflicted with this debilitating disease know it's a slow but sure way to cripple.

However, Sue was a fighter and survivor, refusing to lay down and let MS take over her life and destroy it.

She began her own investigation, checking into what was happening to those afflicted. She delved into what was

could acquire. With that accumulated information and knowledge, she began not only to help herself but others.

In that quest, as she went on, Sue became engaged and married, not before letting her husband Ian know what the pitfalls could be for the future. It made no difference to him, he was with her all the way no matter what.

The story of Sue's success is too long to tell here and now, but this we will say, Sue and others with multiple sclerosis, formed what is now known as the Under Pressure Health and Fitness Club in Chelmsford, performing wonders and looked upon with great respect from the medical world on what Sue and her fellow sufferers have accomplished.

The club has members from grandfathers to seven-year-old boys, who looked to a gal called Sue to defeat what has before been called a disease that finally gets you down in spirit and body.

The Lash has followed Sue's determination, faith and progress for these past years, and he is in sheer wonderment of this lady who has braved all kinds of difficulties, illness, and disability to overcome MS.

Along with her fellow members at the fitness club, what great admiration they must be given for their salvation for a better life and achieving it in the face of adversity.

So as you can read, the Lash is one of Birmingham Sue's fans, and also so overjoyed, that she has a normal family life, doing magnificent things for others and most of all

■ THE beautiful lady on the left standing next to Sir Freddy Laker is Sue Cornell, known in days of yore as Birmingham Sue. The Lash writes of this brave and gallant lady in today's show.

Whenever the Lash feels down in the dumps, he just thinks of that very special person, Sue Cornell, with her inspiring courage and achievements over, as we say, adversity and he says right "pick yourself up, dust yourself off and start all over again", and doing that, you know something...it works.

Birmingham Sue, carry on darling, you're winning.

Leaving the bar one night, my friend Frances and I decided to get a taxi home. The trouble was that, as ever, we had very little money, so when George dashed out and offered to share our lift, we were only too happy to let him.

He can pay, he's got more money than us, we both thought, as he tumbled into the back seat.

"That's great, girls, thanks for letting me share," he said, before dropping the bombshell. "I hope you've got the money." My friend and I looked at him, completely dumbfounded.

"We don't have any money, we thought you did!" I said. George shook his lovely head.

"No, I never carry money." He had to dash back into the club and borrow the taxi fare. Clearly, there was always somebody around willing to pick up the bill if you were George Best. It was that sort of life: fluid, fast and glamourous. I'd met Frances after I had been seeing a guy on the island, a French DJ called Patrice who was a big name in Majorca and had his name in lights on the Barbarella nightclub sign. One weekend he said he couldn't see me for a couple of weeks as his girlfriend was coming over from England.

Frances was that girlfriend, and she later became his wife! We got on so well that we ended up sharing an apartment together (and have remained lifelong friends). Meanwhile, my life of glamour continued. I had frequent invitations for lunch with Frankie Vaughan and his wife and other celebrities

Leave it to Georgie 'Wolfman' Best, Northern Ireland's greatest footballer, to get some giggles out of dee-jay Birmingham Sue when she broadcast over Radio Mallorca, Channel 96.6FM live and direct from the (MOP), My Own Place, other-wise known as Riki's Bar.

George Best with me live on Radio Majorca in the Majorca Daily Bulletin

George Best and the manager of Sergeant Pepper's Nightclub

Patrice, Sonia (flatmates and go-go dancer) and a waiter at a nightclub in Palma Nova

My friend Frances

like Sir Bernard and Lady Docker, who came into Ricki's often. Sir Bernard was chairman of BSA in Birmingham, who I used to work for. His wife was a 1960s socialite 'It' girl: when she was in town, everyone knew. Larger than life, she craved attention, and whenever she came to Ricki's Bar she insisted that Ricki take pictures and put them in the *Majorca Daily Bulletin*. She adored champagne, fur coats and extravagance. It is said that the Daimler car bears a mascot modelled on her naked body.

One night, Gilbert O'Sullivan came into the bar. Ricki hadn't noticed him, despite me trying to get his attention to tell him, so I started playing Gilbert's music. Gilbert nodded in response, and that's when Ricki noticed him. We worked as a team whenever celebrities came in, getting them the recognition they desired. PJ Proby invited me out to dinner, and I took him to a nightclub, El Rodeo, owned by a friend of his who was in the group Los Bravos. I also met a guy called Graham Godley who came in with Lol Crème; they were members of the band 10CC, which had just broken up, and they were about to go solo. Noele Gordon, an actor from the soap *Crossroads*, would come to the bar and chat to me. Mum would have been so proud because she always watched *Crossroads*, but I couldn't phone her and tell her so I had to delay all my celebrity news and put it in letters.

One time, Ricki asked me to go and talk to a girl my age who had come into the bar with her father. She was using a walking stick. Her name was Beverley Patience and her

Me, Tommy Docherty, Lou Edwards and other board directors of Manchester United

father was Bob Patience, who owned The Barn restaurant in Braintree. A bungled robbery had taken place and Beverly had been shot in the back, while her mother had been shot and killed. The total value of the safe's contents had been taken, a mere £90 for the cost of a life and the ruination of another. Beverley sat with me and talked about what had happened. (I met her again after I was married, in a restaurant in Braintree. We recognised each other and struck up our friendship again.)

After Ricki's bar closed in the early hours of the morning, Sue, Sandra, Frances and I would meet and go across the passage to the nightclub Jack El Negro, where a local Spanish band, Los Valdermosa, played. When the nightclub Babbles, next door to Ricki's, opened at 3am, we would move on there.

Me and the officers from the JFK Aircraft Carrier

Me, Chely and Franciosa

It was a strictly private members' club, but I was Birmingham Sue and everyone knew me, so I was allowed in. Rod Stewart was a frequent customer too. From Babbles we would then go on to Barbarella or Sargeant Peppers or to Plaza Gomilla, where the 'in crowd' would congregate. At that time in the morning, the local bakeries opened, and we would buy ensaimadas for breakfast or go to a local café at 5am for a Majorcan dish of rabbit and rice. This would finally be the end of my day, and I would go back to my apartment to sleep until noon before work at the *Majorca Daily Bulletin*, where Ricki would put together his column about the celebrity guests we had seen in the bar the night before. He had a section in his column called 'True or False', with embellished stories about the characters who had come into the bar.

Back then, the John F. Kennedy aircraft carrier was stationed in the Mediterranean to help deal with the situation in the Middle East. It would make frequent visits to Palma and dock just outside the bay for a few days at a time. It was an impressive sight, all lit up. We would certainly know when the sailors were in town, as all of the nightclubs would be full. I avoided the clubs then. The officers found their way to Ricki's, and together with my friends Frances, Sue and Sandra, I was invited for tours of the JFK ship. It was a real privilege because the general public wasn't allowed on board and we were treated with great respect.

While I was working at Ricki's, I was invited to a birthday party by my friend Steve Draycott, where I was introduced to a good-looking Spanish guy called Chelly. Five years older than me and suavely dressed, I was smitten when he kissed my hand. Steve teased me.

"He's a bad guy, keep away from him," he warned. But this only made me even more smitten! Chelly treated me like a princess and came into Ricki's on many occasions, much to Ricki's annoyance. He took me to Ibiza and even gave me a key to his apartment, so that I could come and go as I pleased. There was a real spark between us, but I knew that because of his lifestyle I would never feel secure, so I could never commit myself.

My career as a DJ flourished on Radio Majorca, Channel 96.6FM. Ricki had made me a celebrity, and had even hung a watercolour painting of me by a local artist in the bar. Being from Birmingham had its benefits. I did interviews, music and commercials and worked for Ricki's paper, the *Majorca Daily Bulletin*. Everywhere I went I was recognised and feted. However, as I was about to discover, this also had its downsides. After a time, a particularly handsome nightclub owner called Pepe took me under his wing.

"All respectable girls have bank accounts," he told me. I didn't, and was surprised when he deposited £50 in my name to open a new account before inviting me for lunch at his apartment. My excitement quickly turned to fear when I arrived: he closed the door behind me and locked it. Heart pounding, I asked to go to the bathroom, pulled myself through a skylight window and ran away as fast as my legs would carry me. I had a lucky escape and learnt a vital lesson: to trust my gut feeling when it came to decisions and danger. I never saw him again and never touched the £50 in the bank account.

Ever the grafter, in any spare time I had I would help Ricki put together another small weekly newspaper, the *Town Crier*, which he launched with a photo of me from my modelling days on the cover. (Long after I'd gone, people would return from their holidays in Majorca and tell me they'd seen me in Ricki's column in the *Majorca Daily Bulletin!* My celebrity status was international, right up to his death a few years ago!)

Inspired by Tony Blackburn's Radio One show, I asked Ricki if I could put on a live request show. He agreed, and installed new equipment and a tape-recording machine so that I could take requests from the holidaymakers in their hotels. The show became so popular that people would come into the bar and ask for Birmingham Sue with their requests.

One day I turned up and the windows in the bar had been broken, and all the equipment stolen. The police believed it was an inside job as the windows had been broken from the inside and no one could scale the outside cliff face.

"I'm sorry Sue, I can't afford to replace the recording equipment that was taken. We'll have to shelve the request show," Ricki told me. Maybe it was Ricki's way of making sure my own show didn't become more popular than his 'Ricki Lash Show'. Fame's a fickle thing.

La Semana Mallorquina

MAJORCA TOWN CRIER

SUE MILLS IS SPAIN'S ONLY ENGLISH—SPEAKING GIRL DEE—JAY ON RADIO MALLORCA.

IS DEAN MARTIN'S SON A REBEL? TURN TO PAGE 7.

FAT LAST STRIKES AGAIN ON PAGE 10 & 11. TRUE OR FALSE?

RITA WINN HAS MADE IT IN FASHION IN MAJORCA. TO SEE WHY, TURN TO PAGE 9.

With time, the glamour was slowly beginning to fade. Whilst I was still very happy to live in that world, which had satisfied my inner need, I began to realise it was an unreal world. A plastic environment, where everyone was 'on show' 24-7, performing a part to the outside world – myself included, even though I worked hard, at the newspaper in the afternoons and as a radio presenter for Ricki at night.

Despite the lifestyle and being surrounded by serious party people, I had never succumbed to alcohol though. I didn't actually drink very much at all. Ricki even concocted a special fruit juice 'Susie Special' cocktail for me that one of his many friends, Tony Appleton, a carpet shop owner from Essex, always insisted on buying me.

So when I got up from my regular tea time nap in the apartment at 7pm to get ready for my radio job one night and suddenly collapsed, my legs completely buckling from under me, there could be no question that I was drunk. Even if I looked it. As frightened and bemused as I was, I was determined to get to work, even when my body refused to respond properly. The show must go on. Struggling all the way to Ricki's clinging onto any support I could find en route, I must have looked like Bambi taking his first steps on the street.

"I don't know what's wrong with me. My legs gave way completely, I've had to walk all the way here hanging onto the walls," I explained as I apologised to Ricki for my lateness.

The show did go on, and afterwards Ricki arranged for my friend Steve to drive me home. Waking up the next morning, I was fine. As good as new. There was nothing wrong with me or my legs. Little did I realise that my sudden collapse was the first sign of things to come. Life as I knew and loved it was about to drastically change direction.

5

IN THE DRIVING SEAT

I t's a warm, balmy evening at the end of May 1974 and I'm pulling up outside The Retreat pub in Chigwell, Essex, in a car that attracts almost as much attention as that yellow Lotus Europa did on Kitts Green Road. Only this time there's a major difference: I'm in the driving seat now and it's my very own company car that's the head turner. My life really has moved on!

At the back of my mind in Majorca, I knew that at some stage I'd need to return to real life and a real job with real money. So here I was in Essex of all places, after trusting my gut instinct and, purely on impulse, leaving Ricki's bar (and a farewell note to Chelly) to fly back to Heathrow in February. Landing with no money and no job lined up, my prospects were limited to say the least when we touched down on the tarmac. Too proud to go back to Birmingham in the circumstances, I'd arrived with my suitcase on the doorstep of my friend Steve's sister Sue, who lived in Seven Sisters, north London. She and her husband shared a one-bedroomed apartment with their new baby, but kindly offered to put me up initially if I slept on the sofa. I accepted gratefully, only to be kept awake at night by mice nipping at my toes!

Falling back on my old secretarial skills, I enrolled with the Alfred Marks Bureau 12 hours after landing. Pride soon restored, I rang my mother from my first temporary post, sitting in the Lord Mayor's dark, dreary office in London overlooking Big Ben, to tell her I was back in Britain. In comparison to the interesting and glamorous life I'd lived in Majorca, however, it was very dull, so I asked for a transfer and was sent to work on The Mall. (Which is where I was when a gunman shot and wounded four men in a kidnap attempt on Princess Anne just outside Buckingham Palace.

Leytonstone High Road in 1974. The orange sign is the art and craft shop we lived above

Although we didn't know anything until we watched the TV news reports.)

Weeks later, I was offered a permanent job with cigarette company, John Player Special, as part of their promotional team. The position came with a company car and a transfer to Cardiff. It was a great city and I met many interesting drivers, like James Hunt. I even considered moving there to work as part of the John Player Formula One team. Then, out of the blue, my mother rang with a message from Frances to ring her. In doing so, I discovered that she'd left Patrice behind and returned, like me, to Britain. Frances's father had bought an art and craft shop in Leytonstone High Road, London. She had a flat above the shop and wanted me to share with her. Perfect timing as I'd just been offered an interview with Carreras Rothmans as a full-time sales representative in London. Purposely driving to the interview in my John Player Special car to demonstrate my experience, I got the job. Rothmans had begun to employ women on an equal salary to men, with a company car, expense account and clothing allowance. Amazingly rare for those days! When asked where I'd like to be based – London, Birmingham, or Cardiff – I chose London so that I could live with Frances. It was all coming together again. And here we were: me at the wheel and Frances in the passenger seat of my lovely white Hillman Hunter, emblazoned with the Rothmans blue stripe logo. It was a car to die for – and a real man magnet!

That night at The Retreat, it was the subject of cars that engaged Ian Cornell and me in our first conversation. He'd been one of a gang of four guys looking over at Frances and me as we ordered drinks at the bar. Eventually they came over and began chatting. Ian grabbed my attention when he mentioned that he'd just got back from Monaco and was going to Le Mans. Being a car lover, I was impressed.

This guy's quite exciting! I found myself thinking. *There's something about him. He's different…*

When he told me he came from Essex, I cheekily retorted, "Where's Essex?"

It turned out that we knew some of the same people, like Tony Appleton, who'd bought me all those 'Susie Specials.' After closing time, they came back to our flat for coffee and as they left, Ian, who'd been sat on the floor with me, asked for our phone number at the flat.

"Who's he going to ring?" asked Frances.

"I've no idea. I hope he rings me!" I replied. "You've got Patrice in Spain!"

Two days later the phone rang and Frances answered it. It was Ian ringing for me!

I've won! I thought smugly. Only to be let down before too long…

Agreeing to a date, Ian drove me to a pub where we met his friends. Feeling comfortable with them, I took it as a good sign. I just liked his personality. He didn't brag; he was a gentleman and, all in all, very lovely.

I'll keep him around, I promised myself – even though, at the time, I was seeing the guy who was training me at Rothmans.

Soon afterwards, Ian told me that he was going to the British Grand Prix and wanted to take me with him for the weekend. Thrilled, I agreed, only to be let down at the last minute in a Friday night phone call.

"I've got a busy weekend and I can't go," he lied.

"That's absolutely fine," I snapped back.

But inside I was gutted – and absolutely furious. Whoever you are, you just don't treat people like that. No person does that to me. Being the first of only seven women on the Rothmans sales force, I had female friends to go out with. I was particularly friendly with Della Burt, the ex-wife of the pop star Heinz, who was a member of the Tornadoes, famous for their multi-million-selling record Telstar. And I was also surrounded by 200 men. There were plenty to choose from if I wanted a date. Even Chelly was still hanging on, writing, begging me to return to Majorca and be with him. I certainly didn't need or want a man who would let me down. For the first time in my life I was in the driving seat. And you didn't mess Birmingham Sue about.

6

HERE FOR LIFE

Arriving at my hospital bedside, fresh from a birthday weekend with his friends in Devon, I can't help but feel that Ian has something important to say to me. As I lie there, pondering what it can be, the green hospital screens are suddenly whisked around us. Maybe the nurses, sensing the need for privacy, also share my intuition that something's afoot…

I was in Barts Hospital after mentioning to Frances that I was getting some tingling and numbness in my fingers. She'd suggested I go and see the doctor, and as we had one right across the road in Leytonstone, I had gone for a consultation. The doctor had thought I was just run down.

"You just need a tonic," she advised. I duly took one, but after three months the symptoms weren't going away and I'd gone back to see her.

"I keep getting this tingling and I keep tripping over," I said. "I'm not walking very well, I'm getting so clumsy I could trip over a matchstick!"

"Oh, now I'm a bit worried," she said. "I'll send you to Barts to get checked."

Barts is one of the oldest London hospitals, established in the 12th century on West Smithfield in east London, and it had become the main teaching hospital for the newly formed City and Hackney Health District – a forerunner in research. It's still an imposing building, with views of St Paul's Cathedral nearby. I was admitted as an inpatient, thinking that I would be in for just a couple of days.

By now, Ian and I were very much back on. All was forgiven and forgotten regarding his broken promise to take me to the British Grand Prix: he'd managed to track me down at work a few days after leaving me in the lurch. I'd taken his call in the Rothmans training school.

"I'm really sorry," he'd said, before telling me he'd gone anyway. As had I with my own friends.

"That's absolutely fine," I retorted, secretly impressed by the effort he'd made to find me. So when he asked, "Can I see you?" I'd agreed to give him another chance to prove to me that he was the man I'd thought he was.

The first time he picked me up, he'd been driving a hired estate car while waiting for his new one – a Ford Mexico – to arrive. That meant nothing to me, and I wasn't impressed until I saw it on our second date. Black, gold and sleek, it was the car of the moment and is now a collector's item. Funny how cars have always marked important events in my life. Over the years I've even named my pets after them

– from Ferrari to Porsche, Bentley and even Picasso, as in Citroen!

We'd only been out a few times when I very, very casually mentioned that I'd some tingling in my fingers and that I was going to Barts for tests, and that I might have to stay for a couple of days. In my own mind I had convinced myself there was nothing to worry about.

"Don't worry, I'll come and visit you," he said. Those few days turned into a few weeks and Ian visited all the time, which was good of him considering our relationship was still fresh and new. The tests were inconclusive to begin with, and my life settled into the hospital routine. I'd been put on a geriatric ward and was well enough to chat to the other patients, to walk around, help the nurses and make the tea.

By now, it was obvious to me that Ian was The One. I'd always known I could trust my gut feeling. I was so confident about our special relationship that I'd even taken him on his first trip to Birmingham to meet my family. He obviously felt the same way because one night in a car park in the Hawk pub at Battles Bridge, he'd told me he loved me.

At my bedside now, he was telling me how much he'd missed me in Devon and giving me a little rock sculpture with a beautiful painting on it that the artist had signed. It's still one of my most prized, and priceless, possessions to this day.

Mine and the nurses' hunch was right, and he hadn't even got out those four important words – "Will you marry me?" – before I was cutting him off mid-sentence in my excitement to answer, "Yes!"

Despite being the most unromantic setting for a proposal, it was such a beautiful moment. The nurses were almost as excited and emotional as we were. Some of them were even crying. I was the happiest girl in the world.

What I didn't know at that moment was that my decision to accept Ian's marriage proposal would be the last truly free decision that I would ever make. Even as we celebrated, storm clouds were brewing over our future...

The first person I'd phoned with my exciting news was my mum, and a few days later she turned up with my gran, her own mother. I was surprised and perplexed that they had come to visit, but I was pleased to see them. What I didn't know at the time was that Barts had contacted my mum and asked her to come down. She was my next of kin and they wanted to tell her what they had found out. As soon as my new fiancé came in to visit, she took him aside, out of my earshot...

Quite soon after my discharge, Ian became distant. He'd make excuses not to see me or change plans to meet up and discuss arrangements for our wedding. I thought he was distracted – perhaps he had someone else? I talked it over with Frances as I couldn't understand his sudden change of heart. Frances spoke to Ian, but she couldn't get anything out of him either. So one night, I challenged him: "What's wrong? Have you got someone else?"

It was time for him to confess.

"There's no one else in my life," he promised, holding me close, 'but you've got an illness. I've been told not to tell you, but it's really difficult for me and I can't keep it a secret any longer. I have to tell you, Susie. You've got MS." I was stunned. I didn't even know what it was.

Slowly, it all started to become clear. Apparently in her conversation with Ian at the hospital, my mum had revealed something that she thought it was his right to know...

"I've just been told that Susie has MS," she'd announced. "It's a lifelong condition and the doctors have told us that within three months she could be in a wheelchair."

Perhaps she'd wanted Ian to know what he was taking on; it was unlikely that she'd been trying to scare him off, but she knew it was right for him to know. And it was. But it was also right that I should know too.

Apparently, the hospital had said that I was not to know and to carry on as if everything was normal. That's how it was in those days. They discharged me and signed me off to go back to work with a doctor's note that said I had Polyneuritis, something I'd never heard of. I believed that it was the correct diagnosis as my symptoms had gone into remission. The doctors said that I should carry on as if life was normal. Little did I realise that life for me would never be normal again. How could life be normal? What did the hospital think I would do if they told me the truth? As it was, they kept me in the dark. I was helpless, which is what I never wanted to be.

Like me, Ian had no idea what MS was and his reaction was one of total ignorance. The disease meant nothing to him. It was a shock to hear that his fiancée could end up in a wheelchair, but at the time he did not believe that it could happen. Now, of course, I know that the current medical diagnosis of multiple sclerosis declares an immune-mediated process, in which an abnormal response of the body's immune system is directed against the central nervous system – the brain, spinal cord and optic nerves. The inflammation damages myelin, the fatty substance that surrounds and insulates the nerve fibres, as well as the nerve fibres themselves, and the specialised cells that make myelin. Messages within the CNS are altered or stopped completely, causing a variety of neurological symptoms that include deterioration of mobility, hence my limping and the sudden lack of use of my legs. But this was late 1974 and MS was not commonly diagnosed – it was a relatively rare condition. There was no Google to refer to, no literature available; our family copy of the doctor's encyclopaedia was out of reach, and there was no one to ask. All the hospital had told my mum and Ian was that I could end up in a wheelchair within three months and that there was no treatment. It was terrifying. I had never felt so frightened in my life, not to mention totally alone. I remember going to the local pub on Leytonstone High Road with Ian and Frances. We tried to act normally, but to me everything was a blur, completely unreal.

This could not be happening to me. Life changed in an instant. I was frightened and desperately sad; I felt that I was being punished for something I had done, some sin I had committed, or for a life lived too fast and furiously. I felt like my whole life was being taken away from me and that I was in a hopeless situation. It was a very low point for me, and I even considered suicide. I went back to Barts to ask for help, but they said there was no reason to see me as there was nothing they could do. My symptoms were in remission, and I should go back when I felt I needed to. As if I didn't need to then! No help, no cure, no hope!

I developed a limp, which alerted the attention of friends and colleagues who wanted to know what was wrong. Those I chose to confide in about my MS looked so shocked and devastated. Unable to cope with their reactions, I quickly learned to say that I had had a fall while skiing instead. I could cope with their reaction to that news.

Left feeling ashamed and unworthy, it was my turn to become distant with Ian as I processed the shock. I could not believe that there was any reason why Ian would want to be with me, why he would want to marry someone who could become a burden. I tried to send him away.

"Don't waste your life on me. I don't want to be a burden. I'm not getting married," I insisted. I felt that this man deserved better. I loved him far too much to put him through all that uncertainty and fear.

But he wouldn't go, and there was no arguing with him.

"I'm here for life," he lovingly promised. "We're in it together. We're getting married and you are going to be my wife."

'Maybe it's not always about trying to fix something that is broken. Maybe it's about starting over and creating something better.'

7

FOR BETTER, FOR WORSE

Holding onto my dad's arm, I am floating down the aisle in a fabulous, daisy trimmed dress and huge veil borrowed for the occasion from my mum's sister, my auntie Janet.

It is the 22nd February 1975 and, after much persuasion, I am marrying Ian in the biggest, flashiest church we could find, the beautiful St Martin in the Bullring, right in the centre of Birmingham.

The day itself is everything I've ever dreamed of, since I was a little girl watching the hundreds of people gathered outside that same church waiting for the bride and groom to appear. I thought that people who got married in there must be very important. Perhaps they were princes and princesses?

And here am I, feeling like royalty myself as I am wedded in holy matrimony to the love of my life. For better, for worse; for richer, for poorer; in sickness and in health. Ahhh. There's the problem. Being diagnosed with multiple sclerosis has been devastating for me, and it's taken a great deal of effort on Ian's part to make me realise that I am still worthy. Luckily I've never been the type to give in, so we've become the Happy Couple, enjoying our Big Day in an amazing church thanks largely to my mum, who knew people through her work as a florist and pulled a few strings for us. I had to be living near the church for the banns to be read, so for months my 'official' residence was The Ship pub nearby, which is where we head for our wedding reception prior to a honeymoon in Stratford upon Avon, staying in the Shakespeare Hotel.

Dad helping me with my dress and veil

St Martin Church in the Bullring, Birmingham

Ian and I on our wedding day at St Martin Church in the Bullring, Birmingham

Settling happily down into married life, we both carried on working – me for Rothmans and Ian for his dad's engineering company. Any spare time was spent decorating and furnishing our first new semi-detached home. We were busy people. Thankfully, my MS symptoms seemed to disappear. I was on the pill because we didn't want to start a family too soon, though we'd agreed it was something we both wanted when the time was right. From the age of 12, when my two younger sisters came along, I'd spent lot of time around babies and couldn't imagine my own adult life without them.

So after our first year of marriage, we decided it was time for me to come off the pill. Naturally, we'd always assumed that I'd fall pregnant immediately. As far as I was concerned, everything was fine; there was no reason why I shouldn't have a baby. Except it didn't happen straight away.

And every month, I would sit sobbing on the loo in our avocado-green bathroom when my period started like clockwork. Then I'd dry my eyes and not even let Ian see how upset I was. I kept it all to myself. It was awful. Meanwhile, all our friends were getting married and having children, meaning I had to smile and look happy for them. And I was; I really was. But inside I was crying. Yet, ever the optimist, I refused to accept that it wouldn't ever happen.

After six months of trying, I went to see my GP who asked if we were 'doing it right' and referred us for tests. The tests were done, and we were told that the likelihood of us ever having children was extremely low. This was a huge blow for us. We wanted our own family to make our life complete.

Life had turned on us and I felt I couldn't endure another disaster. We tried to move on with our lives, going on holidays, decorating and becoming godparents to our well-meaning friends' children, as if they recognised how much love we had to give. We'd even acquired a cute black and white kitten, who we called George. I can see my little sisters now, pushing him round in their doll's pram. He was my baby. The only one I had.

It was taken for granted by our friends and family that we couldn't have children because of my MS, so I continued to let them believe this. By the time our second married Christmas came around, we decided we couldn't face it; me sitting under the tree I'd so carefully decorated willing for there to be lots of baby presents under it the following year. So we took off to Germany for a holiday, and on our return, I realised: "Oh-oh! I've missed a period..." I knew it was odd for me, but on the other hand the doctor had warned that it was highly unlikely that I would ever get pregnant.

Back then there were no over-the-counter pregnancy tests, so I had to go to my GP, where it was confirmed. I was two months pregnant. Needless to say, we were ecstatic. It was beyond belief. We'd defied medical science! It was nothing short of a miracle. We told that the world and everyone in it was thrilled for us. Feeling fine, I carried on working, thrilled to feel the first flutter of our baby in my stomach.

But returning home one evening when I was five and a half months pregnant, I felt a really sharp pain, which was immediately followed by a gush of water. I didn't know what to do, but Ian called 999 and an ambulance arrived to take me to St John's maternity hospital in Chelmsford. We waited and waited and waited and were then told our baby had died. I didn't even have to go through any kind of labour. Everything had disappeared naturally. I was given a 'scrape', and after 24 hours I was discharged, empty handed. We didn't even know what sex our baby had been. And there was no reason they could give us. Medical investigations could only begin if there were two further miscarriages, we learned.

Luckily, I hadn't bought any baby paraphernalia so there was no empty cot or pram waiting at home; nothing to remind me of my loss. My mum, who lived 200 miles away, had always said she never bought anything until her babies were born and, at the age of 25, thankfully I still listened to her advice.

The news destroyed us. Deep down, we knew that a pregnancy might never happen again. We just held on to each other, knowing there was nothing to say. There were no medical answers. Maybe counselling would have helped but none was offered. Once again, we were on our own.

'An angel wrote in the book of life my baby's date of birth, then whispered as she closed the book "Too beautiful for earth"'

8

HUNGARY AND HOPE

Answering the phone, I immediately sense the urgency in the voice of my sister, Yvonne, who's on the other end.

"You have to see the treatment, Susie. There must be something for you!" she gushes.

It was 1988 and I was, in my late 30s, at the lowest point of my life. My MS was getting worse and I felt completely abandoned by the medical profession. My chances of becoming a mother were getting slimmer with time, even though we'd spent thousands of pounds on IVF at Dr Patrick Steptoe's clinic after learning of his pioneering work with Louise Brown, the first test tube baby. He had never worked with the infertility problem we had, so ours was then a unique case. And despite undergoing a total of four programmes, none of them had worked, including a stay of two weeks at Bourne Hall with other women who were going through the same thing. It was good that we were supporting each other, and perhaps that philosophy lodged in my subconscious the idea that there is hope for everything with support and love.

The hope my sister was offering wasn't for babies though; it was for my MS. After my miscarriage I'd taken time off work and decided it was probably time I started to look after myself more. Ian was running the family business , his father having died, and it was doing well. He invented the pickle fork, which appeared on TV on *Tomorrow's World*! So we both agreed that we could afford the drop in combined salary. Despite taking things a bit easier, I started to notice that I couldn't walk on grass, which baffled me. With nowhere to turn for advice, I had to accept it and just avoid grass or walk around the edges of it, holding onto Ian's arm. Strangely, though, I could keep my balance on rocks, as we discovered on a trip to Devon during which we visited some caves. But when we returned home, I fell to the floor while trying to get out of bed one morning and couldn't walk. Crawling to the phone, I called Ian for help. The next morning my legs worked normally again. It was just like that time in Majorca. Based on our past experiences, there didn't seem any point turning to the medical professionals for help. It had taken me years after my MS diagnosis to realise that there was no medical cure. I was on my own; there was no white knight in shining armour.

As time had gone on, my condition was deteriorating. We'd been approached to open a new venture, an advertising agency. Ian would be the financier and I'd

Annabel, Debbie and Chloe. Models for the Prelude modeling agency

utilised my previous experience as a model to set up my own modelling agency within the business. We called it Prelude and it was based in South Woodham Ferrers. There were two other directors and a graphic artist on the advertising side, and I looked after the models. I'd loved doing all the training, showing them how to walk correctly and driving them to photo shoots. We quickly built up a strong client base, including Falmer Jeans and Loveable bras, and at shoot locations I'd help with the styling and make up. This was during the early '80s, a decade of excess, yuppies and big hair. And in 1985, Ian bought his first Ferrari. Red, of course! I used to drive it all the time, loving being at the wheel, still as interested as ever in cars. On holiday in

Mauritius, we stayed at the St Geran Hotel, where Formula One racing drivers stayed after their races at the South African Grand Prix. Walking through the lobby one day, me clinging onto Ian's arm for balance, we were mobbed by a group of girls who saw my F1 cap and thought Ian must be a driver. Fun times! Increasingly, though, they were being marred by my exhaustion, which caused us to give it up in the end. I was finding it difficult to walk for long periods. Some days, no matter how much I tried to pace myself, it was impossible to shower and wash my hair in the same day. A flareup of MS would happen at any time, and to me a 'flareup' meant not being able to walk for a couple of days; when they died down, I couldn't do as much walking as before. When my friends were going on long walks or doing any kind of physical activity, I just made excuses. My legs had deteriorated and my limping had become worse. Just walking up the stairs would exhaust me, and everyday tasks were draining. I had barely enough energy to move, my mobility was becoming much more limited and my left leg became very, very stiff. These physical symptoms left me feeling very low, and I was desperate to find a way to manage the condition, desperate to find help. So Yvonne's call was of immediate interest...

Me in my Ferrari hat

At the age of two, my nephew Ben was diagnosed with cerebral palsy, which affects movement. At the age of three he was accepted for treatment at the Peto Institute in Hungary. Andras Peto was an experienced neurologist and a pioneer in working with children with cerebral palsy, using a holistic approach to overcome any difficulties connected to their neurological motor disorders. The centre in Hungary used the grounding of his work to prove that despite the damage, the nervous system still possessed the capacity to form new neural connections, an ability that could be mobilised with the help of a properly guided teaching and learning process, through a method called Conductive Education.

Spending six months there when Ben was being treated, Yvonne had noticed that a lot of adults at the Institute were walking like me. She couldn't understand what was wrong with them and couldn't ask because of the language barrier. Hungary was still a communist country and quite isolated from the West. Barely anybody spoke English at that time. Finally, through trial and error, she was able to establish that these patients had MS, and got straight on the phone to me.

Ready to seize any glimmer of hope, Ian and I hurriedly packed and found a flight to Budapest, where I turned up at the door of the Peto Institute with my sister. We couldn't speak Hungarian, but through sign language and the eventual help of a translator, we managed to communicate my desire for treatment.

The Peto Institute in Hungary

"Stay here and we will help you," they said. It was the first time anyone had said those words to me. I was overjoyed. Here was hope and help. I was the first British adult to be given a place at the Institute.

I immediately moved into a flat with Yvonne, her daughter Holly and Ben in Budapest. I stayed for three months, and it was hard for us all living in a communist country with a completely different lifestyle. But it was especially hard for Yvonne, as we all relied on her. She had to carry Holly up four flights of stairs, lock her in the bedroom and come back down to pick Ben up and carry him up the stairs, then come back to help me. There was no lift, and no one else to help.

When we went shopping, we had to queue like the Hungarians, and we could only buy what they had, and they had little. Nothing was marketed or advertised, everything was in brown paper packaging. We went to the beauty salon for a treat and it cost us about £5, a week's salary for a Hungarian. When the first McDonalds opened in Budapest, there was a queue a mile long. I watched groups of people, three deep, staring longingly into shop windows at goods they could not afford. We lived a basic but happy life there, and the people were very welcoming and friendly. They were well educated, study was highly regarded and it was very cultural. We didn't have a television; there were no books in English and we were constantly aware of Hungarian guards watching us with suspicion whenever we went anywhere. But it was a small price to pay for the help I received.

At the Peto, they told me that 10% of my mobility problems were because of MS and 90% of the problems were because I didn't know what to do about it. Doctors in the UK had been telling me to rest for the past 15 years. Through this rest, I had neglected the use of my body. It really was a case of 'use it or lose it', and I had lost so much mobility. The Peto said that they would help me manage my condition through exercise and therapy. I gained so much strength from them. I'd been feeling an acute loss of identity, believing that people liked me because they were sorry for me. The Peto changed that. Suddenly I was back in control of my life again.

The Institute was a beige building, a hard shell of brutalist architecture that looked imposing, but inside there were large, clean rooms with tables and equipment and it was light, bright and hopeful. I was put into a small group of adults in a room lined with slatted wooden beds, where we undertook a guided exercise programme that lasted for an hour every day. We would repeat leg raises, throw and catch balls and work with all our muscle groups to strengthen them. The Peto aim was to show individuals suffering from injuries to the central nervous system and their families the way to a full life and to make society aware of the opportunities to help. Conductive Education was available in the UK, it had been introduced around 1969; however, I had never come across it before Yvonne took her son to the Peto. It fascinated me, and I vowed to carry on the exercises when I returned to the UK.

One day at the Peto, Yvonne noticed that an English TV crew from TV AM was coming in. Chatting to them as they were filming Ben, she told them about the adult side of the Institute and her sister who was having treatment there. They had had no idea that the centre treated adults and were surprised to find an English woman there. They were keen to meet me. The Peto gave them permission to film the adult programme and TV AM followed my progress, which publicised the fact that Peto had a programme for MS and Parkinson's. It was to completely change my life and the lives of so many others…

'I can't tell you when, but I can promise you it will get better, it will get easier, and it will all be worthwhile. Just promise me you won't ever give up.'

9

BRINGING HOPE HOME

Strapped into my plane seat while flying back home from Hungary, I am struck by one overwhelming thought: the answer, in the absence of a medical cure for my condition, lies in my own hands and not with the medical profession who'd so readily cast me aside.

Little did I realise just how important that realisation was. Not just for myself but for all those others who, like me, felt there was no hope for their MS and that their lives too were no longer within their control.

Back on British soil, my first port of call was the TVAM studios, where I had been been invited onto the morning show to talk about my experience at the Peto Institute. And suddenly I was on a roll to help myself and hundreds of others heal and cope.

After my appearance on national TV, I was immediately inundated with letters and phone calls from people throughout the country who were feeling as desperate as I'd been. I'm proud to say I answered every one – including all the letters in longhand, which took me ages!

Between answering the letters, I'd started to do some exercises with a local charity, CHARMS (Chelmsford Action for MS), of which I was a founder member and for which I later raised thousands of pounds. We even had people queueing outside the door after having seen me on TV, and I realised that I needed to help more people. So, with help from the local press, I put together a video, the MS Fitness Programme, which was later bought by most physio departments in hospitals throughout the UK.

The idea was that I could reach more people with videos and promote a healthy and active way of living, turning the negative experience of diagnosis of a chronic illness into a positive one and showing people ways to manage their health holistically. I also realised that the more I helped others, the more I was helping myself. It was the first time people could access this sort of exercise at home. The video was the first of its kind, and it sold worldwide.

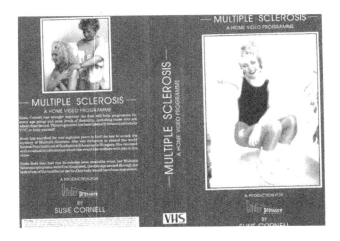

Multiple Sclerosis Home Exercise Programme

I was reading the national magazine *Here's Health* on a regular basis and had become increasingly interested in natural medicine. The magazine was looking for the Health Achiever of the Year, and I entered, thinking that it would be good way of getting my work with MS noticed. I never thought I would win, but to my complete surprise, I did. I was given the title in 1989 at a glamorous reception in the Savoy Hotel.

Health Achiever of the Year, 1989

'Sometimes the smallest step in the right direction ends
up being the biggest step of your life, don't hesitate
take a step.'

This unexpected achievement led to huge national and local press coverage. I was giving interviews and writing articles for national newspapers and appeared as a guest on radio and television programmes. Health specialist Jill Palmer gave me a full page spread in the *Daily Mirror*, and I was in the *Daily Mail*, *The Sunday Times* magazine, *Woman's Realm* magazine, *Chat*, *Bella*, and *Best* magazine. I was also asked to take exercise classes at the famous Pineapple Dance Studio in London.

I was asked to do talks at the MS Society in Londonderry on many occasions, and I took all the names and addresses of interested people afterwards. At first, I was surprised to be told just their first name and the name of the village they were from.

"It'll find me," they would say confidently. Everyone seemed to know everyone there!

Meanwhile, I'd read about a doctor on Harley Street called Bryan Lambert, an Australian osteopath who had started an unconventional exercise course at his clinic using 'machines under pressure' for people with MS.

"Sounds like we're on the same wavelength," I mentioned to Ian. I was interested to know more and keen to become one of his patients, so despite my stiff leg, which had now led to me using a walking stick, I drove myself to his clinic. At £200 a session, it wasn't cheap, but Bryan was the only person in the country offering this treatment.

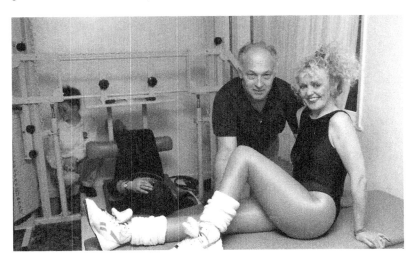

Brian Lambert at his clinic in Harley Street, 1988

Entering his clinic, I was met with an array of weightlifting machines suited to the best bodybuilders, an old-fashioned leg press and an instrument nicknamed 'The Bonker' (before that word had another meaning!) that looked like an enormous leather lollipop. Bryan administered blows to his students that delivered a jolt to the central nervous system, before working in a harness, much like a combination of Pilates and chiropracting today. Through the sessions I began to learn so much about how the body works. Bryan's belief in the body's recuperative powers inspired me to think how I could make his technique accessible to others. I was learning so much about the mechanical workings of the body. I'd already realised how good reflexology was. Surely, it had to be a better, more natural solution to taking medical drugs for a condition nobody understood. Bryan stayed at our house many times, and when he returned to Australia, Ian built a replica copy of his pressure machine in his engineering factory. It was a 10-tonne machine similar to a reformer bed used in Pilates, which we installed at the end of Ian's offices in a room no bigger than a garage. Bryan's patients soon started coming to me from all over the country. I just wanted to make this exercise available for everyone, and to help others the way I had been helped.

Multiple Sclerosis programme spawns 'gym of the future'

Editor Keith Dixon at Chelmsford's Under Pressure gym

"Under Pressure" is a gym like no other in Britain. Launched initially to cater for the needs of multiple sclerosis sufferers, it has developed a unique success formula tailored to attract the reluctant majority of the population which might otherwise be intimidated by the prospect of joining a "normal" gym.

Now husband and wife team Susie and Ian Cornell are looking to offer their expertise in a franchise package.

In particular, they challenge local authority fitness centres to look at their mode of operation and to invest ratepayers money into catering for the majority of the population.

Says Cornell "Not everyone is one of the youngish, fairly fit, beautiful people who tend to frequent most fitness centres. What we have done is identify and cater for the bulk of the population who are outside of that description.

"We haven't created a niche. Its always been there. Its just that we are making the older, unfit person feel comfortable in the 'Under Pressure' environment.

● The lay-out is open plan and completely flat, with an attractive green and tangerine decor. There's a stair lift to the second floor.

● The refreshments area, under cheerful parasols, is right next to the exercise area, so that members can take a break for a rest or a chat whenever they fancy and sunbeds and saunas and relaxation.

● The cardiovascular equipment, by Nautilus and to Row, has been specially chosen for the quality of their graphics, which helps prevent boredom in people who are not used to working out.

● And the resistance machines are supplied by Scandinavian leaders HUR. They are all air pressure machines controlled by discreet valves, so that no one other than the user is aware of the resistance on the machine, thus removing feelings of inadequacy.

● If you doubt how

Susie and Ian Cornell.

Work Out

January 1994
Please Turn Over

Numbers grew rapidly, and it got to the point where too many people needed my help. I had to do more, so I started exercise classes in a room at the end of my husband's factory. I qualified as an ITEC practitioner and lecturer in reflexology, aromatherapy, sports injury therapy and nutrition, so that I could help people further. Word soon spread and we outgrew the room near Ian's offices. Ian had an empty factory unit opposite his office, so he moved our under-pressure machine in there, and we added to it, building a new gym and a new place of pilgrimage for people with MS – as well as many without any illness, who just wanted motivation to exercise. We named it Under Pressure.

The official opening was carried out by Anthea Turner, who was on television a lot at the time presenting *Top of the Pops*, (this was prior to her *Blue Peter* days). We'd met her completely by chance on a beach in St Lucia, where Ian and I were holidaying. Recognising Peter Powell as he soaked up the sun, I asked Ian to go over and say hello to the best friend of my old posh boyfriend in Birmingham. We had a great reunion. Anthea Turner was his wife at the time and we soon got along very well, realising that we shared a lot of similar experiences. Like me, she had been through IVF, and she always thought of me as a great listener. She felt she could always come to me for advice as I'd been through so much myself.

And sadly, another trauma was to come…

10

A SECOND CHANCE

Staring down at the obvious blue line, I quickly dismiss the idea that I can possibly be pregnant.

"It must be a mistake," I confidently tell my friend Anita, who bought me the test after I'd mentioned to her in passing the previous day that my periods had stopped.

"I must be in the change," I'd added.

"Or you could be pregnant!" she'd laughed. I'd laughed too.

"You must be joking! At my age? I've waited over 20 years, it's not going to happen now," I'd replied, thinking that I couldn't possibly be expecting our longed-for baby at the age of 44. It was far more likely that I was going into the menopause. Whilst we'd never completely given up hope of having a family, Ian and I were coming around to thinking that it may never happen and, as such, had just bought two Bichon Frise puppies, Porsche and Bentley. And of course we loved our 10 godchildren – Toby, Sophie, Lucy, Michael, Stephen, Emma, Esme and Leigh – as our own.

But Anita had insisted that I should do a test, which, unlike last time, were now available over the counter. And the next morning she'd handed me one. So here we were...

And to my complete surprise, it was reading positive. Thinking it couldn't possibly be right, I did another test and then another. But they were all giving me the same result. A follow-up trip to see my GP confirmed that the tests were indeed correct: I was four months pregnant. Ian and I were ecstatic. We couldn't believe our luck. It as was if we'd been offered a miracle; a last chance of happiness. A child of our own was all we'd ever wanted after the overwhelming sadness of our last, lost baby.

Tests showed that our precious baby was healthy and that everything was progressing well, so we started to share our wonderful news with all our friends and family.

At five and a half months, I happily went along with Ian to the hospital for a routine scan. But as I was being scanned, the sonographer became very quiet before quickly disappearing to get a doctor. Something wasn't right here. Why did she need someone else? With a thumping heart, I stared tearfully at Ian. We both knew in that instant that our baby had died. This time, the pain was unbearable. Too much. How could this happen again? How could we be shown a glimpse of complete happiness to have it so cruelly snatched away?

It was beyond belief. Ian and I were heartbroken that our little miracle had died inside my womb at exactly the same stage as our last baby. I was detained and given an injection in my tummy to induce the labour. And at the end of the pain and pushing, I was told by the midwife, "It's OK, we've got the baby now," before she took our baby son (who would have been James) or daughter (Charlotte) away. We never knew the sex. There was no funeral. Nothing. All we had left to remember our fledgling child was one scan picture, which I barely looked at again.

It wasn't the first time we'd been through this, of course, but it was so much worse now because of my age. Nevertheless, we traipsed back to the clinic of Dr Steptoe and tried another couple of attempts at IVF, to no avail. Our arms were still empty.

Years later, I learned that our last lost baby was still close to us in the nicest possible way. Without telling me, on Millennium Eve, when we were having our new bungalow built, Ian had buried the scan photograph in a time capsule among the foundations, along with a photograph of the two of us. Our baby's memory will live on in our home as well as our hearts.

'We couldn't wait to hold you and now we can only hold you in our hearts.'

11

DIGESTING NEW INFORMATION

Silently observing Dr Paul Sherwood at work in his Harley Street clinic, I watch bemused as he asks his young patient to open his mouth wide so he can look down his throat.

What on earth is he doing? The child, a 12-year-old boy, has turned up for his appointment with a knee problem!

Once he's finished, Dr Sherwood declares his diagnosis. The child's tonsils are infected, and the bacteria is travelling around his body and, finding a weakened area, is setting up home in the knee injury, preventing it from healing. The boy just needs to have his tonsils removed, he informs the mother.

This was the first time I'd heard of bacteria travelling around the body. I was amazed and in awe of this man. I'd learnt the mechanics of the body from one Harley Street doctor and I was now learning the biochemistry of the body from another. Dr Sherwood – who'd written the books *The Heart Revolution* and *The Back And Beyond* – had agreed that I could sit in on his clinic.

I had already begun to research the links between the immune system and digestive disorders, and knew that Adelle Davis, an American author and nutritionist, said that all health problems start in the gut. One of my own worst symptoms was restless legs and muscle spasms; I often said, "I would give one million pounds to anyone who would cure my muscle spasms." They were horrendous. They stopped me from sleeping and going to the cinema, and long car journeys were difficult because I had to keep standing and stretching my legs. My theory, based on what I'd read, was that many MS sufferers had problems absorbing food, so I found the combination of digestive enzymes and antioxidants improved my digestion and stopped my muscle spasms.

Knowing how little I'd been told about MS when I was diagnosed, I now knew that I needed to put all of my findings together. And what better time to do it than when I was grieving for my second lost baby? I had to channel my grief into something creative and turn the cruelty of loss into something good. I needed to put everything into words. I had to write my book. The book that emerged was *The Complete MS Body Manual*, which I hoped would inspire others and act as a practical guide for people living with MS. We self-published it in 1996 using the gym name Under Pressure for the publishing company. Anthea wrote the foreword and Dr Sherwood wrote the preface. That same year, I was carried in my wheelchair by a team of 14 to the top of Mount Snowden in Wales to raise awareness and funds for MS charities.

The Complete MS Body Manual, *1996*

Today, we estimate that there are 100,000 people living with MS in the UK and that a further 5,000 are diagnosed every year. Worldwide, more than 2.3 million people have a diagnosis of MS. In the United States a recently completed prevalence study, funded by the National MS Society, has estimated that nearly 1 million people over the age of 18 live with a diagnosis of MS.

My book was followed by another video in 1999: *Mission Ability*, with Anthea Turner, which talked about exercise and the effect of digestion on health. In it I announced: "Welcome to my world, where I believe that good digestion and a positive mental attitude can overcome many conditions life has to throw at us. I know, having had to overcome this myself having had a debilitating illness." This growth of experience and expertise led to an invitation to lecture to ION (Institute of Optimum Nutrition) students at Surrey University, with Ian handling the slides, and in a four-hour lecture on a weekend for students, alongside the work of Patrick Holford. We were invited back and gave several lectures over the years. Students were keen to know all they could about MS, and my experience was the perfect gateway for them to learn more about the illness. At this time I found I was needing my wheelchair more and more, and was finding driving more difficult, but it didn't stop me from giving the positive side of what you can do instead of what you can't do. I enjoyed giving people my knowledge and experience, especially when I discovered the bioresonance programme - a scientific programme used by NASA.

'Bioresonance Energy e-Lybra is an energy balancing system that can be used to harmonise imbalances in the person's bio-field and help bring the body back to its natural state of balance.' Victor Simms WDS

Me and Anthea Turner

Mission Ability, *an exercise video for people who can't exercise*

It's perhaps more accurate to say that it found me: a rep for the company walked into my office looking for me, explaining that she'd been sent by a doctor who felt that I could work well with it. She opened her briefcase and then proceeded, quite unwittingly, to blind me with science!

In my nutrition work, I was already using the Vega Machine for testing food intolerances and imbalances. However, bioresonance uses distance consultations and treatment and is a system of listening to the body, looking for imbalances within – which can be physical, spiritual and emotional – and feeding back from this for treatment and healing. It is very efficient for treating physical pain, which may be a locked in emotional trauma, and is especially efficient at helping to treat complex conditions like autoimmune disorders. More research and practise convinced me that it was the medicine of the future, and today I use a machine called e-Lybra, which runs with a computer programme that can be accessed remotely, enabling me to treat clients from all over the world. e-Lybra scans the body for imbalance and looks for energetic remedies to rebalance the cause of a person's symptoms.

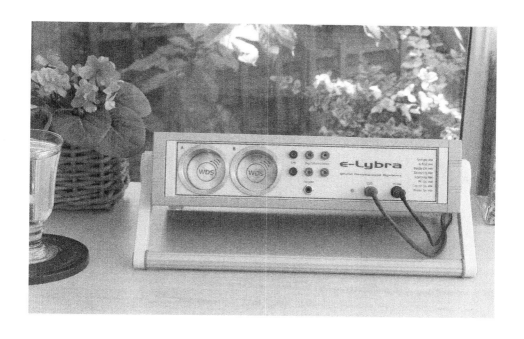

Anthea also featured in a BBC radio documentary about my work, which was introduced by the late Alvin Stardust. Word continued to spread, as did journalistic interest: Joan Bakewell came and did an interview with me in the room where we had the pressure machine, and I was in *The Sunday Times Magazine*. It was while I was reading this that I came across another article about my old friend, Freddie Laker, and his wife, Jacquie, who had been diagnosed with MS. I got straight on the phone to Ricki in Majorca and told him I needed to get hold of Freddie. He gave me his direct number, so I rang him up and said told him it was Birmingham Sue. He remembered me, and I told him that I had MS and that I could help Jacquie. He flew her out to the UK; she stayed with us up at the house and I was able to give her the support she needed. The two became frequent visitors, and on many occasions when we were out, total strangers would come up wanting to shake the hand of the man who revolutionised the airline industry by offering the first budget transatlantic commercial flights

The gym increasingly provided accessible exercise for all. It was the first inclusive exercise place for people with mobility and health issues. We built frameworks and installed weights and pressure machines, static cycles and other specially adapted equipment, including a bank of white and turquoise seats that looked like the bridge on Star Trek. It was space age for its era, and proved to be extremely popular. We had over 800 members, as well as a beauty salon and an MS clinic which attracted people from all over the UK. We produced a cinema advert for the gym, which ran for 18 months at our local Odeon. Ian wrote the words, I did the backing vocals and a friend, Bobbie Harrison, who was the drummer for Procol Harum, sang the main vocals. The stars of the advert were our staff and gym members. Today it's on YouTube!

Alongside the gym we opened an ITEC school and I qualified as an ITEC lecturer, following the International Therapy Examination System, and had students come from all over Essex. We attended a star-studded ceremony in Stratford upon Avon, where Under Pressure was awarded the Best Health Club in the Country by the Fitness Industry Association. I was given their Lifetime Achievement Award for integrating exercise for everyone. Ours was the first gym in the country ever do this.

Receiving the Lifetime Achievement Award from the Fitness Industry Association

The gym had attracted interest from other health organisations and, seeing our success, bigger national companies started offering similar facilities. We couldn't compete on that scale, so Ian sold the membership to another club, and all our members were absorbed into that. I wanted to continue my research and work with MS sufferers, so we negotiated rental on a room for my own work. Knowing that I was setting up this facility, their receptionist at the time, Karen, asked if she could come and work with me as my work looked more interesting. She came onboard and she's still here.

For 15 years, all was going well until I turned up at the club one day to find it locked and bolted and a man with a set of keys outside. Devastated by the death of Ian's mum, we'd just left the funeral parlour, so the news that the club we rented rooms from had gone into liquidation was the last thing we needed to hear. I could not continue to run my clinic there. With typical resilience, Ian urged me not to panic. Believing in the power of positive thought and that there's always a way of turning a setback into an opportunity, we decided to convert the garage of our home and we opened the clinic there. The Cornell Centre was reborn.

12

STARS AND CELEBRITIES

Answering a 9am knock at the door of our Florida hotel room, we're surprised to see a smiling man wearing a uniform and a flying hat. The badges on his lapel show he's an airline official.

"Freddie sent me," he explains.

Freddie was the wonderful late Sir Freddie Laker, who'd become a good friend through my helping Jacquie with her MS. To celebrate his 80th birthday in 2002, he was throwing a party at his place in the Bahamas. And he'd invited us!

By this stage, I was in a wheelchair, which I'd been using on a regular basis since the late 90s. Not bad considering that that was more than 20 years after doctors had predicted that it would happen within weeks! We'd bought a bungalow in Chelmsford in 1999 and I was still able to get around holding on to furniture and the walls. However, using a stick for my mobility was affecting me because I was finding that I couldn't walk long distances. I was trying to trick myself into thinking that a little bit of the rest would help. Ian would jokingly refer to me as 'Jake the Peg' to help me laugh off my immobility. My friends just accepted me as I was, and I constantly had to hold their arm to help me balance.

During the move, we'd had to seriously consider my future mobility, and had switched to an automatic car, which meant it was easier for me to continue driving. That was important to me as my mum was still in Birmingham and I could drive to visit her, relying on her to help me out of the driving seat at the other end. Sadly, my dad had died years ago, when I was in my 20s, after he and Mum had parted for a second time.

Travelling by plane to the Bahamas was rather more difficult on this occasion, as we'd arrived in Fort Lauderdale, Florida, too late to get a connecting flight to the island. Airline staff had said that as I was in a wheelchair, there was no room for us.

"But we have people waiting for us in the Bahamas," we'd wailed, before ringing Freddie, who told me not to worry,

"We'll get you over," he'd promised.

And true to his word, here was a man ready to whisk us off in a private jet to the Bahamas. We landed on a deserted runway and were led to a shed in a field! While we waited, a three-wheeled van like the Reliant Robin in *Only Fools and Horses* came screaming up the runway, emblazoned with 'Laker Airlines'. Freddie was driving it. Somehow, he got us in and took us off to his house, where the front garden was his yacht and the back garden was the ocean.

Freddie and Jacquie made such a fuss of us; he treated Ian like a son. They would often go off together to look at his yacht. Freddie kept a secret bottle of rum in the cupboard on board, so they went to look at the yacht quite often! His garage was full of memorabilia from the now-collapsed Laker Airlines, and he told us about his number plate, 'F1'. He was constantly on the phone to Richard Branson whilst we were in the house: he still had his finger on the pulse and loved his airline. In the Bahamas everyone knew him, and he was treated like a king. We attended his birthday party with SkyTrain staff, met his son, daughter and friends and were treated as part of the family. He later died, but we are still in constant contact with Jacquie, who still lives in the Bahamas and manages her MS quite well.

The Lakers weren't, by far, the only celebrities we encountered on my mission to help people. So many were benefiting worldwide from my work following the Peto-influenced exercise programme, the gym, books and videos. Through it all, I'd come to the conclusion that MS is caused by a breakdown in the immune system caused by emotional or physical trauma and poor digestion in the gut. I noticed that two to three years before their first symptoms, clients at my consultations had had an emotional or a physical trauma. When I looked back on my own life, I realised that my own emotional trauma – my break up with John – happened two years before my first MS symptom arrived. At the time, I'd dealt with it in my own way, not talking about it and overeating comfort food. I'd never put the two things together before. My work was published in a natural health magazine and I was quoted by Lyne Mactaggart (editor of *What Doctors Don't Tell You*) as the first person to put leaky gut and multiple sclerosis in the same sentence. She published my work, which meant that it reached even more people in need.

As I changed the lives of others, my own was changing too. It was taking me down some very interesting – many glittering – paths.

I'd had an idea in the early '90s to acknowledge people who were facing adversity. I had started to receive some recognition and awards myself, including a very prestigious civic award from Chelmsford County Council, and similar recognition for my work. Sandra, a headmistress friend, had asked me to present awards to some pupils at her London school. Awed by what these children had achieved, I realised that there were so many other children out there caring for others who were not receiving any recognition. Inspired, I thought there should be an awards scheme in Essex for people who had achieved so much. Unsure where to go with my plans, I turned to the editor of the *Essex Chronicle* and asked if he'd help me. Together, we launched the first Achievement Over Adversity awards in 1993.

With the help and sponsorship of the Ford Motor company, I was able to take the award scheme throughout the UK, going to cities like Aberdeen, Leicester, Exeter,

Hull and Nottingham. We were on the front pages of most newspapers. Then we lost the sponsorship from Ford, so we decided to concentrate on promoting the achievement of people in Essex. These awards metamorphosised into The Pride of Essex Awards, which are now in their 26th year.

Me and Sir Cliff Richard. We talked about digestive enzymes

Me with Her Royal Highness the Countess of Wessex at the Achievement Over Adversity awards

Some of the most moving evenings of my whole life have been the times we've hosted these special awards, supported by sponsors and celebrities such as Anthea Turner, Alvin Stardust, Terry Waite, Bob Champion, national footballers and Rick Wakeman. Humanitarian and former hostage negotiator Terry Waite presented the awards in 2000. HRH the Countess of Wessex has also presented these awards.

It was through my work and famous new contacts that I continued to meet inspirational and famous people in my personal life. It was at Anthea Turner's wedding to Grant Bovey that I met Alvin Stardust, who was sitting at the same table in the huge marquee. We got on straight away. Apparently he thought I was fast, witty and full of fun! He expected me to leap up and start dancing as soon as the music began, and was shocked to discover that I couldn't, as I was in a wheelchair. Alvin later happily supported

The Pride of Essex Awards, and we were invited to his daughter's christening. Ian and I arrived at the church and were surprised to find so many celebrities there. Cliff Richard was the godfather and was a close friend of Alvin. At the reception, he came and sat with us together with his manager and the Radio One DJ Mike Read. It was a pleasant afternoon spent swapping stories. I'd met Cliff before when we were dining at The Ivy in London with Anthea, Grant, Gloria Hunniford and her husband. Cliff talked about digestion and I discussed digestive enzymes with him. Ian was convinced that Cliff Richard copied his hair style!

Me and Rick Wakeman

As used to sitting with celebrities as I was, I was still overawed when I received a telephone call from Debbie Rowe, the photographer for one of the magazines I'd been featured in. She was putting a book together and wanted me to be a part of it.

Me and Alvin Stardust, around 2002

"You're the first name on my list. You inspired me so much when I took your photographs," she kindly told me. It was a book about 50 women over the age of 50 throughout the world, women who had achieved extraordinary things. My story sits among that of women such as the world's first Spitfire pilot, the original calendar girls and the Hollywood actress Susan Sarandon. The book launch was held in the Houses of Parliament, where I met these inspiring women, who'd been flown in from all over the world. What an honour it was to meet them – particularly the wonderful actress Virginia McKenna, star of the '60s blockbuster film Born Free and founder of the wildlife charity the *Born Free* Foundation.

extraordinary women, extraordinary lives

Debbie Rowe & Tricey Larcombe

50 Over 50: Extraordinary Women, *launched at the Houses of Parliament, 2007*

Me with Virgina McKenna

It wasn't all glamorous work and play though. On one occasion I found myself in Pentonville Prison! One of my patients got involved with handling drugs. He was looking for pain relief, and cannabis provided this. At the time, the medical use of cannabis was still illegal, and he was unfortunate enough to be caught buying some for personal use. His solicitor asked me to be a character witness for him, and Ian and I travelled down to London to be present at his court case. We gave evidence on the reliability of his character and about his condition, which was multiple sclerosis. He was still given a jail sentence of 18 months in Pentonville Prison.

His solicitor wanted him out of there: as an MS patient on crutches he was suffering, it wasn't the right place for him to be. The solicitor asked, "Could you go and do a physical examination, a health assessment, on him, please, Susie?" I had never done such a thing – I wasn't a qualified doctor – but I agreed to help. I took Bill, who worked with me, as my 'physical therapist'. The prison believed I was a doctor. Bill pushed me in my wheelchair through their security – they didn't even check the briefcase on my lap or my handbag. I entered Kenny's cell and the guards shut the door, leaving me alone with Bill, my 'therapist', and Kenny. The first thing Kenny asked for was a pen – it would be worth a lot of money to him, as pens were used as currency in prison. He also asked if I had any cash on me and promised to repay me. I knew Kenny, he was my patient and I trusted him, so I gave him my housekeeping money. He was eternally grateful, and he did repay me once he was out. We chatted for a couple of hours; there was no need to do a physical examination: the condition of the prison said it all. Afterwards I wrote an official letter to the governor, recommending that my patient be relocated, that Pentonville was not the place for him. The governor looked at my report and my patient was transferred to Chelmsford, so that he could continue having treatment with me on a daily basis. He was now my responsibility!

Kenny arrived for his first appointment in a police car with a guard in full uniform. He got out of the car in handcuffs and on two walking sticks. How did they think that he was going to run off? It was quite laughable. Ian stopped them in the car park.

"You can't come into Under Pressure dressed like that, you will frighten people away," he told them. So the police took their hats off. On following visits, they came in with no jackets, and eventually Kenny's wife would pick him up from prison and take him back. In the end his family and friends were allowed to visit him as long as I got him back to the prison after his programme. He stayed under my care for 12 months and was eventually released. He and his family were eternally grateful for our help and we have all remained friends.

Despite my innate love of all things ritzy and glitzy – and there's no denying that the awards dip me back into the fabulous lifestyle I enjoyed in my 20s, with their glossy ceremonies and free flowing champagne – I've never lost my main focus or forgotten who the real stars are. And that's the immensely brave people who are nominated for awards and those who are, without complaining, battling their own problems.

**'Live to inspire, and one day people will say,
because of you, I didn't give up.'**

13

BY APPOINTMENT OF HER MAJESTY THE QUEEN

S taring at the envelope routinely handed to me by the postman one morning in 2004, I noticed that it was emblazoned with the lord lieutenant's crest. Curious, I ripped it open and let out a scream when I read the contents.

Dear Susie,
Her Majesty the Queen has given me leave to appoint you
Deputy Lieutenant of Essex.

Not even knowing what this was, I telephoned the lord lieutenant who had sent the letter, Lord Braybrooke, formerly of Audley End. I had met him some time before to ask if he would come to the Achievement Over Adversity Awards, and he attended for a couple of years.

Lord Braybrooke congratulated me on a very prestigious position. It was an unbelievable feat of achievement, and one of the pinnacles of my life. The lifetime title has given me the power to open doors, to achieve what is important to Essex and the people who live there.

It's also had its amusing moments over the years. My role means that I have stood in for the Lord Lieutenant of Essex at events and, as such, you are the Queen's representative, seated where the queen would be, addressed as Ma'am as the queen would be and given the same protocol as Her Majesty. There aren't many women deputy lieutenants in the country and assumptions can be made, as I found out when I was sitting next to a very upright colonel wearing a monocle at one formal dinner.

"My dear, how long has your husband been a deputy lieutenant?" he asked.

"He's not. I am!" I replied. He was so surprised that he actually dropped his monocle into his soup!

I was one of the first female deputy lieutenants in Essex, and Essex has now appointed the first woman lord lieutenant since the office was established in the 1500s. Times change. Who would have thought that a girl from Birmingham who didn't even know where Essex was would become deputy lieutenant of that same county? I feel very privileged.

I was also given the title of Member of Court at the University of Essex, and I enjoy the wonderful opportunities to explore the work of the university. This role has enabled me to mix with businesses, lecturers and students, working towards improving communication about the university.

My awards pinnacle was reached in 2007. Ian rang my office and said that there was a letter from the Prime Minister, Tony Blair, for me. Should he open it? I couldn't contain my excitement when I opened the letter and read that I was being awarded an MBE from the Queen. I was overjoyed. My medal was presented by the Prince of Wales at an investiture in Buckingham Palace. I had met him before at the Health Writers' Awards in the Reform Club, London, when he'd asked about my work in natural medicine, and he remembered that we'd met when he gave me my MBE.

Me with His Royal Highness the Prince of Wales at the Reform Club, London, around 1999

My husband Ian, my mother and my mother-in-law Mary accompanied me to Buckingham Palace, and we went on to celebrate with lunch at the Houses of Parliament surrounded by more family and friends. If only my dear old dad could have been there…

Receiving my MBE in 2007

14

STILL IN THE DRIVING SEAT

As soon as the morning light streams through the bedroom curtains, my daily routine begins with a quick senses check.

Opening my eyes, I am relieved to find that I can still see. The sound of running water tells me that Ian is in the shower, and that means that I can still hear. A quick wiggle of my fingers reassures me that I haven't lost the sense of touch, and a call to Ian lets me know that I can still speak. All's well!

When you've had MS for 45 years, as I now have, you don't take anything for granted, even though my symptoms are stable. My movement is already limited, but I value every single moment and function that I still have. Helped by Ian to shower and dress, I still put on my lipstick, as I always have. A more sophisticated Chanel red has these days replaced the Miners fuchsia pink of my youth!

Unfortunately, I can't sashay into sports cars any more as I'm restricted by my need to use a wheelchair and walking stick. They still dent my pride a bit, but it's not the end of the world. What's a wheelchair if not just another vehicle? I am still firmly in the driving seat! Even if it's not at the wheel of a flashy Rothmans car! I gave up driving on the road some years ago and it was devastating to lose that independence.

Free will is something that I learned is not a right years ago, when I was diagnosed and my choices started to become limited. But I very quickly learnt that if I couldn't change something, I had to look for a way of working with it and get something positive out of it.

My philosophy is that I do not have a disability, I have a gift. Others may see it as a disability, but I see it as a challenge and this challenge is a gift because I have to be stronger to get around it, and smarter to figure out how to use it.

Me at work in my clinic

My way of coping now is to use my decades of experience and knowledge to help others. Like one of my first clients, who came to me after being diagnosed with MS. By providing her with personalised recommendations on diet, lifestyle, emotions and exercise – and more recently, bioresonance – I've enabled her to stay symptom-free. Another client, Wendy, came to see me because she was experiencing pain all over her body, including the soles of her feet. She could not bear for anyone to touch her, and her doctor had put her on antidepressants. When I ran a bioresonance scan, it picked up that her problem was not depression, but the aftermath of an emotional trauma. Wendy said that she had gone through a relationship breakdown 18 months previously and had also lost her beloved grandmother. By not allowing her inner self to grieve, the heartache was showing as physical pain.

Another young client came to see me with symptoms of IBS. A bioresonance scan detected no food intolerances but flagged the colour turquoise – a colour associated with helping people who have been bullied – as important. She revealed that she'd been bullied at school and again, at the age of 20, and was finding university very stressful. Her suffering, we discovered, was due to her difficulty in making friends, which related to her bullying earlier in life. I recommended a natural adrenal support programme, which calmed her emotions and her digestive system.

Barbara was suffering from depression and came to me

for a bioresonance consultation, which revealed that wheat was a problem food for her. She eliminated it for a week, and was astonished to find that her depression disappeared. She was keen to follow bioresonance as she wanted to handle her problems holistically. Barbara found her joint pain ceased and her energy was restored, enabling her to feel confident enough to embark on a new career. While I would not argue that all depression is caused by wheat consumption, how many other causes can be so easily remedied? No prolonged psychotherapy or antidepressants, no electroshock therapy to zap your cerebrum.

Bioresonance is a therapy that can be carried out long-distance, as one of my clients in France testifies. She was diagnosed with systemic scleroderma, and like me with my initial diagnosis of MS, she had no idea what the disease was or how it would go on to ravage her health. It started with swollen fingers, skin tightening in her arms, face and chest, acute exhaustion and rapid weight loss. The hospital consultants suggested medication for kidney transplant patients, which was their only adequate prescription for trying to calm down an immune system that had gone off the rails. She did a bioresonance distance consultation with me in August 2010, and found that I was very accurate in my assessment of her needs. Despite this client's initial scepticism of eLybra, she was impressed by the results. She states that meeting me was instrumental in her journey to recovery; she has made so much progress in her physical and emotional health that even the doctors are surprised. She would recommend my help to anyone with any health problem.

Satisfied and happy clients give me a remarkable sense of achievement and contentment. Life led me down a different path to the one I envisaged, but maybe it's the one the universe mapped out for me – who knows? I don't believe in fate or luck, but I do believe in the power of thought and the benefits of positive energy. And my work isn't finished yet. I will always look at 'beyond what's possible'.

'If you stumble, make it part of the dance.'

15

MAKING IT LOOK EASY
A LAST WORD FROM IAN

Behind Susie's dazzling smile, there's a real vulnerability that few people know about. It's born from living with a medically incurable illness and it's what connects her to the clients she so desperately wants to help.

If you saw her at a glittering awards do with her red lipstick on, you'd probably never guess that I'd helped her to shower and dress because she can't do it herself. That's the image Susie likes to portray: one of hope, inspiration and resilience. Life must go on and disability mustn't get in the way. The mantra 'Smile and the world smiles with you. Cry and you cry alone' was written for Susie.

Her philosophy has worked not just for her, but for MS patients all over the world. She refuses to take no for an answer and helps them to do the same.

But the downside is that Susie has a habit of making it all look so easy. And I would hate readers of this book to think that that is the case. Because it isn't. No disability or incurable illness is easy when you're living with it day to day for years on end. Just travelling with a wheelchair – whether by road, air or sea – can be fraught with difficulty, and society has a lot yet to learn about accessibility. So too had one hospital when, after an operation, staff didn't know how to lift her out of bed without a hoist.

As strong as she is, the emotional and physical anguish Susie's had to endure at times is unimaginable. That's particularly true of one occasion, years ago, when a respectable-sounding woman in Dubai offered her a natural 'cure', and we invited her and her two dogs into our home. Six months later I had to practically evict her: she'd made all sorts of wild claims about working with Susie in a bid to snatch her clients, contacts, expertise and good name. The last straw was when she told Susie she would never be rid of her MS while I was around! It was a learning experience, and one that would never have happened had Susie not been so vulnerable and desperate enough for a cure that she trusted the wrong person. Susie doesn't promise vague cures, she promises holistic, scientifically based help and healing to cope. All with a big infectious smile. And we all love her for it.

Oh, how I wish your arms,
your touch would be more than a kiss
To move around the floor holding you tight,
eyes shut, no one insight
Oh, how I wish to dance, how lovely that would be
to dance to see you moving free.

Ian Cornell, November 2019

Susie and Ian

AFTERWORD

Enormous thanks must go, as always, to the light of my life, my husband Ian, for his enduring love and support. They must also go to my cherished friends, colleagues and clients, past and present, who believe in me. I want them to realise how much helping them has helped me. So much more than they will ever know.

Happiness is not experienced in the past or in the future. Happiness is always experienced in the moment. If you are waiting to be happy sometime in the future, you might be waiting a very, very, very long time.

'The secret of health for both the mind and body is not to mourn for the past, not to worry about the future, not to anticipate troubles, but to live the present moment wisely and earnestly.'

– Buddha

Printed in Great Britain
by Amazon